IMAGES OF LONDON

EAST ENDERS'
POSTCARDS

"Night Walks,"
Kent Street.

"CHAMBERS." GRAY'S INN.

"A SMALL STAR IN THE EAST."
RATCLIFF HIGHWAY.

"Wapping Workhouse."
The Saracen's Head. Aldgate.

"Shy Neighbourhoods,"
Punch & Judy.

"Shy Neighbourhoods,"
Brentford.

"Two Views of a Cheap Theatre,"
A Death's Head Pipe.

"Poor Mercantile Jack,"
The Norwood Gipsey.

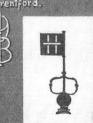

"City of London Churches,"
St Peter's Golden Key.

"Wapping Workhouse,"
Commercial Road.

"Chatham Dockyard,"
A Pope Joan Board.

"Shy Neighbourhoods,"
Whitechapel.

"City of London Churches,"
A City Churchyard.

"Wapping Workhouse. Mr Baker's Trap."

"On an Amateur Beat,"
Houndsditch Church.

IMAGES OF LONDON

EAST ENDERS' POSTCARDS

Brian Girling

TEMPUS

London Life – the Piano Organ, *c.* 1910. Postcards depicting street activities and characters in the East End, and elsewhere in London, were popular in Edwardian days when lengthy sets of 'London Life' gave a vivid picture of the capital at work and play. The rich tones of the piano or barrel organ are among the most evocative sounds of old London, and the arrival in an East End street of a player with his jolly tunes often led to scenes such as that shown on this card by London publisher J. Beagles & Co.

Frontispiece: A Dickens Postcard, *c.* 1910. London's East End has provided colourful settings for a variety of fictional works including those of prolific Victorian novelist Charles Dickens. Dickens' characters were popular subjects for Edwardian postcards but this photographic montage of locations from the work *The Uncommercial Traveller* is rather unusual. Among the tiny views are the Saracen's Head pub, Aldgate; Commercial Road; Ratcliffe Highway and Whitechapel High Street.

First published in 2002 by Tempus Publishing Limited
Reprinted 2004, 2006

Reprinted in 2010 by
The History Press
The Mill, Brimscombe Port,
Stroud, Gloucestershire, GL5 2QG
www.thehistorypress.co.uk

Reprinted 2011

British Library Cataloguing in Publication Data.
A catalogue record for this book is available from the British Library.

ISBN 978 0 7524 2494 1

Typesetting and origination by Tempus Publishing Limited.
Printed in Great Britain.

Contents

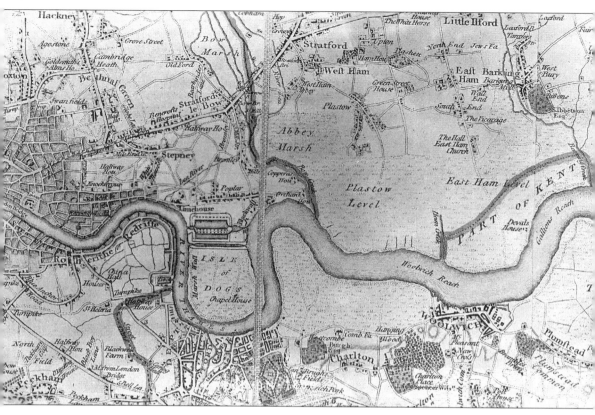

East London, c. 1810. An Edwardian postcard reproduction of an earlier map of the East End with the Thames the dominant feature as it meanders through the flat landscape to the east of the City of London. The first of the docks which were to transform acres of un-drained marshland into the world's greatest port were already in place, but large tracts of what is now the London Borough of Tower Hamlets were still rural in character, and east of the Middlesex/Essex boundary at the river Lea there was unbroken countryside.

Introduction

Imagine a world where there is no radio, television or cinema and where newspapers carry few, if any, photographs. It is a world where few people own a camera and where illustrated magazines are more likely to feature engravings than photographs, It was into this image-starved world, Britain in the 1890s, that an innovation that would change all that began to make a tentative appearance – it was the picture postcard.

There had been plain postcards since 1870 and pictorial ones in continental Europe from soon after that, but the Post Office was reluctant to allow them here until 1894 when the regulations were relaxed. Even then, the first British postcards were far smaller than the ones we know today and the message had to go on the front leaving little room for a picture. Finally, in the early 1900s, the message space was moved beside the address leaving the front free for a full-sized picture – the postcard as we know it was born.

Publishers immediately began producing cards in vast quantities picturing every imaginable theme and competing with each other for the best selling designs, all of which could be posted to anywhere in the country for one half penny, half the price of a letter. A new collecting craze was born and it was the humble viewcard which became foremost in

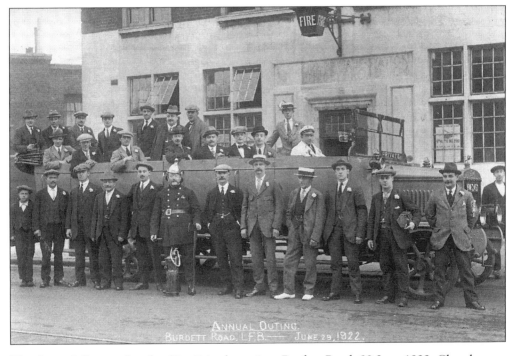

The Annual Outing, London Fire Brigade station, Burdett Road, 29 June 1922. Charabanc outings such as this were popular subjects for postcards which were for the private use of the individuals featured rather than for sale to the public. Here Burdett Road's fire-fighters prepare for some well deserved leisure time.

popularity. The new medium was seized upon by the nations photographers who, freed from the shackles of studio work, set about photographing their localities with a thoroughness which may astonish us today.

Together with popular tourist 'sights' and seaside beaches filled with overdressed Edwardian bathers, everyday town, village and rural scenes were duly recorded for the picture postcard as were local and national events, many images of which had previously been unavailable in any other form. The postcards were often on sale within hours of an event taking place, anticipating the role of illustrated newspapers and newsreels in later years.

Londoners soon caught the collecting mania as postcard pictures of the capital began to appear in countless numbers, but the London, and particularly the East End, the first postcards depicted was a vastly different place to the one we know today.

The Pool of London and the flat Thames-side areas to the east of it were then home to the greatest trading port in the world. Ships were still being built on the river, and the docks, wharves and yards were complemented by an array of businesses concerned with the maritime trade. London's East End extends inland from the river, much of it built in the nineteenth century as the docks expanded and the need to house their workers arose. These populous streets were the cockney heart-lands with traditional local neighbourhoods sometimes complemented by the colourful lifestyles of foreign seamen who had settled and raised families in the East End. Waves of immigrants beginning with the Huguenots 300 years ago also added to the cultural mix in the East End.

By comparison there is a loftier, leafier East End today with the sky-scraping towers of Canary Wharf overlooking a Thames-side newly vibrant with smart river-view apartments and walkways, while inland, modern residential estates have risen on the sites of streets of cosy old terraced houses. Even so, much of the area's traditional community spirit remains firmly in place and the East End remains what it has always been, the very essence of London.

This book takes a nostalgic tour of the three former Metropolitan Boroughs; Stepney, Poplar and Bethnal Green which were amalgamated in 1965 to create the London Borough of Tower Hamlets. There are a few excursions into neighbouring areas and wherever possible, previously unpublished images have been chosen which reflect the life and style of the inner East End rather than its architectural heritage.

Many of the postcards illustrated were produced in the East End while others come from sets of London-wide views. In some cases the postcard message gives added substance to the view with the eye-witness impressions of East Londoners from nearly a century ago. The postcards were all of similar shape and size but where a detail has been selected from the whole, shapes may vary in the book. Photographic enlargements of many of the pictures are obtainable from the author, telephone 020 8863 9194.

One
East of the City

The Tower of London from Tower Bridge Approach, c. 1919. London's historic fortress, former prison and royal residence, has stood at the boundaries of the City of London and what is now the London Borough of Tower Hamlets for nearly a millennium since William the Conqueror began building it in the eleventh century. With its unique and often bloody history, the Tower is London's foremost tourist attraction and its image has adorned countless picture postcards since these first appeared in the 1890s. This example by publishers Degen & Lewis of Nottingham shows the Tower from an uncommon angle – Tower Bridge Approach, with its heavy dockland traffic, still horse-drawn in 1919. This elevated road was built to give the traffic a level run onto London's great Gothic river crossing, Tower Bridge, which opened in 1894. Formerly the river was reached by steeply sloping Little Tower Hill. The postcards of Messrs Degen & Lewis are noted for their highly animated street scenes which wonderfully evoke the London of the years following the First World War.

Tower Bridge from Bermondsey, c. 1895. In common with the Tower of London, Tower Bridge has for over a century been one of London's most popular postcard subjects. This one was one of the first in this long lineage – indeed the bridge had only been open for one year when the card was published, its decorative style being typical of the continental postcards which were forerunners of the British ones.

Tower Hill, c. 1912. An atmospheric early-morning scene on Tower Hill with Tower Bridge seen through the mist and a hazy sun illuminating the horse-drawn wagons as their drivers seek refreshment at Tower Hill's coffee stalls. The outline of the twelfth century Bell Tower adds to the picturesque effect. The postcard is from a lengthy series of sepia tinted London views published by Judge's of Hastings whose founder, Fred Judge, set a high standard of photography with unusual lighting effects and skilful compositions. (Judges Postcards, Hastings).

Trinity Square, c. 1910. This postcard photograph by Park's Press Agency of Fleet Street records a dock union meeting at what has long been a traditional venue for such events. The road to the right was the long-vanished George Street which, when demolished, revealed a most impressive section of the Roman and medieval city wall.

The Crooked Billet (Reilly's), no. 1 Tower Hill, c. 1906. This is one of the lost pubs of Tower Hill occupying the corner of King Street which was renamed Eastminster in the 1930s but has now been swept away. Landlord Matthew Reilly proudly proclaimed that his premises were the 'oldest wine and spirit vaults in London' and this postcard was issued to promote the pub, but poor printing did not do it justice. There is a glimpse of a neighbouring business, that of William Say, cycle dealer whose shop was topped by an elegant Venetian window.

Tower Bridge and the Tower of London, 17 and 18 August 1915. The Tower of London was built to protect London from attacks from the river and the landward side, but the First World War brought a new kind of aerial assault against which it was defenceless. This postcard was published in Leipzig and shows a fanciful depiction of the war in London as seen from a German point of view with a Zeppelin airship cruising unscathed through defensive gunfire as it discharges its bombs over the city. Artistic license has moved St Paul's Cathedral into the scene and given St Katherine Docks a residential riverfront, right.

Aftermath of a Zeppelin raid, Minories by Aldgate High Street, 14 October 1915. It was a night of terror in London as five Zeppelins attacked the capital leaving seventy-one fatalities and a trail of damage which included the destruction of the London & South Western Bank on the Minories corner. The Three Nuns Hotel in Aldgate High Street seen on the left - an 1876 rebuilding of a seventeenth-century coaching inn - lost some windows but looks otherwise undamaged. The scene was preserved on an amateur's photograph which was printed as a postcard.

The eastern City, *c.* 1920. Postcard panoramas like this became popular from the 1910s as photographers took their cameras aloft to record local areas from what were then unfamiliar viewpoints. Here, the eastern side of the City of London is seen with its then low-rise buildings, many of which have now gone. The Roman city wall is unseen here but the ancient street pattern which grew around it is evident as the roads curved round the City boundaries. Visible landmarks include Fenchurch Street station, lower left, with to the right of it Crutched Friars, Jewry Street and Minories running northward to Aldgate. The beginning of the East End and the market area of Petticoat Lane is at the top of this Surrey Flying Services postcard.

Aldgate Pump, *c.* 1912. By popular tradition, the East End begins at Aldgate Pump although it is actually within the Portsoken Ward of the City of London. Aldgate was an access point through the City wall and the Aldgate well was mentioned in the thirteenth century.

Aldgate High Street, *c.* 1905. This early postcard by Stepney publisher Alf Musto shows at the far left the barbers shop which would shortly be rebuilt as the American Bioscope. The Three Nuns Hotel is seen again and, beyond it, Aldgate Underground station as it looked before its reconstruction in 1926.

The Hoop & Grapes, Aldgate High Street, *c.* 1920. This picturesque building is a rare survival from the seventeenth century and can still be found amid the clamouring traffic of modern Aldgate. The attractively coloured postcard was produced by the Photocrom Company, a prolific publisher of postcards in a variety of styles.

Opposite: The Original American Bioscope Exhibition, no. 8 Aldgate High Street, *c.* 1907. East Enders have a long tradition of cinema going which for some would have began here at this, one of London's earlier cinemas. Harry Rosenthal opened his tiny establishment, nothing more than a converted barbers shop between Wattam's Hotel and the Three Nuns Hotel around 1907, charging 1d and 2d admission for a short but continuous programme. By 1908 the 'exhibition' was owned by William Davidson but by 1910 it had been taken over by Popular Picture Theatres Ltd with closure following around 1911. Meanwhile, the displaced barber, Isaac Danziger had moved to the first floor where he continued to provide his 2d shaves and 3d haircuts.

Middlesex Street (Petticoat Lane), c. 1920. The street marks the boundary of the City of London and the former Metropolitan Borough of Stepney, now Tower Hamlets, the street's name a reminder that this was once one of the points were the City of London bordered the County of Middlesex. The East End begins in earnest here with its world famous Sunday street market which dates back some 300 years to the days when French Huguenot immigrants set up their stalls selling petticoats and other garments. This view is of the Aldgate end of the market, which no longer exists following the creation of a vast traffic system, and shows Whitechapel High Street and Mansell Street in the background; the narrow dark entry on the left was Boars Head Yard.

Woolf's shop, Middlesex Street (Petticoat Lane), *c.* 1921. The unique style of the market largely stems from the Jewish immigrants who settled around Petticoat Lane following oppression in their homelands. Among them were the Woolf family who set up shop in Petticoat Lane in 1820 and were still there more than a century later – Mrs Clara Woolf was the registered shop owner when this postcard photograph was created. The shop traded in a variety of household merchandise and included the postcards used in this sequence of market scenes. Neighbour David Leib Ornstein with his dress shop was another of the Jewish businessmen to flourish here – his shop was later taken for an extension to Woolf's.

Petticoat Lane Market, 1930s. A later market view with the Woolf store then owned by Harry Woolf, the self-styled 'Dartboard King'. The postcard was another Woolf publication and features a drawing of a cockney character and a rare example of the cockney dialect to be found on a postcard.

Petticoat Lane, *c.* 1920. Petticoat Lane was primarily a clothes market but in these early views the clientele appears to have been mostly male. The sign 'Hokey King' marks the stall of Joe Assenheim of Stoney Lane with his ice creams – Hokey-Pokey was an old name for the ice cream sold by street vendors. A fur stall like that on the right would attract hostility nowadays.

Street vendor. Petticoat Lane, *c.* 1905. Cockney market traders provide a rich vein of sales patter as they talk up a crowd with good humour and sheer cheek. This splendid gentleman would have sold you a watch in no time at all. The postcard comes from a series of Edwardian street characters called 'London Life' and was published by John Walker of London and Essex.

'Prince Monolulu'. Petticoat Lane, *c.* 1935. Arguably one of the most famous and flamboyant characters to inhabit The Lane was racing tipster Peter McKay 'Prince Monolulu' with his Zulu plumage and familiar cry 'I've gotta horse'. A photographic postcard of unknown origin. (Ann Harris Collection)

'A Whitechapel Sale', Petticoat Lane, *c.* 1936. A photographic study of a market trader in action with a client reaching for his change while others look on. The postcard comes from a series of photographs by the Dr. Conrad Fine Art Publishing Co. whose portrayal of familiar London scenes was distinguished by original viewpoints and a 'candid camera' style.

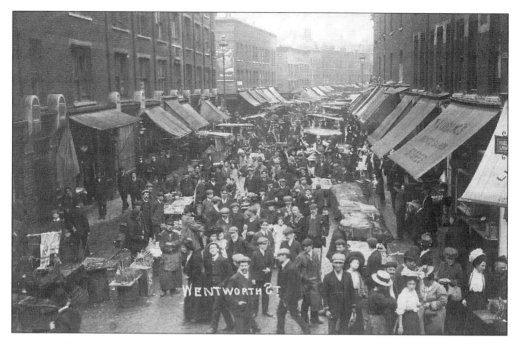

Wentworth Street, *c.* 1905. Wentworth Street runs eastward from Petticoat Lane, and hosts a busy midweek market as is seen on this 'Shadow Catchers' postcard.

Wentworth Street by Old Castle Street, *c.* 1919. A busy scene in the market with its street stalls and Jewish shops. A typically lively study by Degen & Lewis which shows the street before its further part was widened.

Two

The River Thames

London exists because of its river, the great maritime highway which the Romans called Tamesis as they created their settlement of Londinium beside it in the first century AD. The Romans built long straight roads to their town and the river facilitated trade from its heart to the continent. The Romans were succeeded by the Saxons, in time the town became a city, and by the late eighteenth century the world's most prosperous trading port. Dock building began to transform the riverside of eastern London and through the nineteenth century the vast scale of the new developments shaped the East End we know today. This postcard from around 1920 shows the Thames snaking through the capital from Westminster in the foreground to the East End at the top of the picture, with the river's great meander around the Isle of Dogs showing up well. Visible here are the waters of the West India Docks with the Royal Docks in the far distance.

Tower Bridge, the Tower of London and St Katherine Dock, c. 1930. Tower Bridge crosses the Upper Pool of London, a place where maritime trade has carried on for nearly 2000 years since Roman galleys discharged their cargoes here. Victorian prosperity brought the mighty Tower Bridge to replace the inadequate Tower Subway, a foot tunnel which for three months incorporated a cable hauled tram car. To the right of the view warehouse blocks surround one of the basins of St Katherine Dock which was built from 1825-9 by Thomas Telford on the site of the twelfth century hospital of St Katherine-by-the-Tower. The General Steam Navigation Company's Irongate Wharf can be seen beside Tower Bridge, the future site of the massive Tower Thistle Hotel.

Tower Bridge, c. 1920. Tower Bridge's twin bascules are raised to allow taller ships access to the Southwark and City of London waterfronts.

The British & Foreign Wharf, *c.* 1905. Postcards which show working Thames-side wharves are highly elusive but this example by photographers Biddle & Co. is a fine example. The wharf is alive with activity as a cargo of wine and spirits is discharged from a vessel on the river, while on the landward side in Lower East Smithfield (St Katherine's Way), horse-drawn wagons were waiting for the cargo's onward transmission.

Off St Katherine Docks, *c.* 1910. A typical scene on the working river before such activities relocated further downstream in the second half of the twentieth century. This postcard was published and sold in France by Neurdein of Paris where London views were popular.

Sunset off St Katherine Docks, *c.* 1912. Another of the richly atmospheric London views photographed by Fed Judge and printed in a deep murky sepia which does much to emphasise the evenings dank river mists and the looming Gothic splendour of Tower Bridge. (Judges Postcards, Hastings).

The Wapping foreshore, *c.* 1912. Tower Bridge is almost lost in the mist but the entrance to Wapping Basin and London Docks shows up on the right. The houses seen here were built from 1811-13 for occupation by officials of the London Dock Company. (Judges Postcards, Hastings)

Pier Head, Wapping, c. 1906. Dating from 1805, this was the original entrance to London Dock via Wapping Basin. More of the elegant housing for the dock officials is seen here, and beyond them can be seen the Gothic style warehouse at Oliver's Wharf dating from 1870. One of the earliest projects of regeneration which began to transform the Wapping riverfront into an upmarket residential quarter began here in 1972 when the warehouse took on a new role as a luxurious apartment block.

Tunnel Pier, Wapping, c. 1906. The Port of London Authority's Tunnel Pier was named from its proximity to the world's first under-river crossing, Brunel's Thames foot tunnel which was begun in 1825 – it now accommodates the East London Underground railway line. The pier handled passenger traffic on the river including the London County Council's steamboats, but according to the message on this coloured postcard business was not always good, 'we are not to be honoured with a winter service this year as last was such a dead loss to the LCC". The service of 'Penny Steamers' discontinued by 1907.

Wapping Basin, London Docks from Wapping Bridge, c. 1906. Looking into the docks from the world's first cast-iron swing bridge, which was built by civil engineer John Rennie in 1804 to carry Wapping High Street over the dock entrance. The postcard was sent by a local, 'this is where father works'.

London Docks Entrance, Nightingale Lane (Thomas More Street), c. 1906. The main road entrance was located on the City side of the docks with Customs and Excise offices situated until 1840 outside the walls which were then extended to encompass them. The sailing ships of old have since given way to the commercial towers of Thomas More House. This view concludes a sequence of four coloured postcards by Charles Fielding of Watney Street, see page 43.

Sun Tugs, c. 1925. The picture postcard proved to be a highly efficient medium of advertising and publicity and for the price of a half-penny stamp it made an effective 'mail shot'. Tug boat owner William Alexander of St John's Wharf, Wapping High Street used this card to promote the various services his company offered on the river.

The Town of Ramsgate and Wapping Old Stairs, c. 1908. This is a rare survival from over thirty sailor's taverns which could once have been found in Wapping High Street, its name originating from the fishing boats from Ramsgate which in earlier times moored off Wapping Old Stairs. When in the sixteenth century Wapping High Street was laid out on the newly drained Thames-side marshlands, the land was divided into narrow strips, the Town of Ramsgate occupying one of the last of these to still be recognised. Wapping Old Stairs is another historic survival, one of the once numerous access points to the Thames foreshore. Despite the passage of nearly a century, this postcard view appears remarkably unchanged.

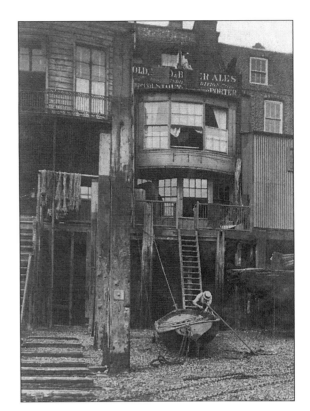

The Grapes, Narrow Street, Limehouse, c. 1910. The site of a pub since 1583, the Grapes gives a rare reminder of the picturesque East End riverfront of yesteryear and forms part of a unique terrace containing seventeenth and eighteenth century buildings. The Harbour Master's house, left, has however been demolished. The postcard gives no clue as to its publisher.

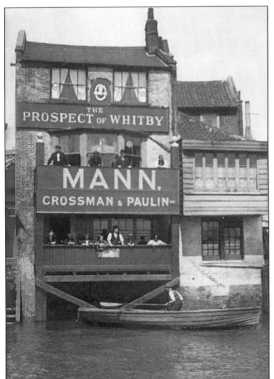

The Prospect of Whitby, Wapping Wall, c. 1930. Another ancient nautical inn, the Prospct of Whitby dates from around 1520 and was formerly known as the Devil's Tavern due to the nefarious activities of the smugglers and thieves who frequented it. It took its present name in the eighteenth century; the 'Prospect' was a vessel from Whitby which used to moor close by. The historic tavern's clientele has included diarist Samuel Pepys, while artists Whistler and Turner drew inspiration from the changing mood of the Thames as seen from the Prospect's windows and balconies.

Limehouse, c. 1925. The riverside hamlet of Limehouse was named after the lime-burning kilns which were there in the fourteenth century, although the sixteenth century saw a busy seafaring community in Limehouse with shipbuilding and associated industries along the river.

London's first canal, the Limehouse Cut, linked the river Lea with the Thames from 1770,and in 1820 the opening of the Regent's Canal connected the Thames to an array of inland waterways from the spacious Regent's Canal Dock at the Limehouse end of it. All of Limehouse's waterways can be spotted in this panoramic postcard by Aerofilms of Hendon, with the Thames off to the right and Regent's Canal Dock (Limehouse Basin) with its coal barges, cranes and wharf-side activities dominating the scene. Limehouse Cut is seen running northwards towards Bromley-by-Bow (centre to top left), with Regent's Canal entering the basin at the left by the railway viaduct. The viaduct was created for the London & Blackwall Railway (originally the Commercial Railway) from 1836-40; it now accommodates the Docklands Light Railway (1987). Limehouse's grand parish church of St Anne (1714), can be seen at the top of the picture, while less elegantly, the smoking chimneys of Limehouse Paperboard Mills at Hough's Wharf appear centre right by Narrow Street which bridges the various entrances to the waterways. The former Regent's Canal Dockmaster's House may be spotted lower right; it was built in 1905 and in 1989 took on a new role as a popular riverside pub, the Barley Mow. The regeneration of London's docklands from the 1970s and 80s has seen the transformation of Limehouse Basin, its waters now surrounded by smart apartment blocks overlooking a lively marina. A new subterranean road, the Limehouse Link now runs beneath part of the old dock basin.

Regent's Canal Dock (Limehouse Basin), c. 1910. A postcard photograph which captures the bustling activities of the basin in its heyday with laden coal barges, a sailing ship and wharf-sides stacked high with cargoes. The scene is overlooked by the Limehouse Paperboard Mills, left, which was founded in the late 1800s.

Limehouse Pier at high water. c. 1906. The pier was built by the London County Council for their passenger steamboat service, an early form of 'river-bus' which ran from Hammersmith to Greenwich. The steamers failed to make money and the service was withdrawn in 1907 but the pier was not removed until 1946.

Aberdeen Wharf with SS *Hogarth*, Limehouse, *c.* 1905. The site of a seventeenth-century shipyard, the Aberdeen Steam Navigation Co. wharf and dock at Limehouse accommodated the company's steamships which ran between London, Aberdeen and other Scottish ports – street access to the wharf was gained from Emmett Street. SS *Hogarth* was named after company chairman Alexander Pirie Hogarth.

Aberdeen Wharf and Dock, Limehouse, *c.* 1905. SS *Aberdeen*, another of the company ships is seen in the dock with a barge which was being used for the transfer of cargo. The Blitz left the buildings in ruins and the site was cleared in the 1980s for the glittering high-rise world of Canary Wharf's Canary Riverside, but a fragment of the old dock entrance can still be seen by the Thames Path. Copies of this postcard were only obtainable from the shop of Henry Hart in Three Colt Street, Limehouse.

Pier Head Cottages, Millwall Dock, Isle of Dogs, *c.* 1905. The Millwall Dock Company's dock on the western side of the peninsula of the Isle of Dogs opened for business on 4 March 1868, with these cottages for company employees being provided in 1875. With their enviable views of the dockside activities, all of the cottages lasted until 1955 and four of them survived until 1986. This fading sepia postcard was sent from an un-named resident of 56 Havannah Street, Millwall.

Millwall Dock, *c.* 1905. The Liverpool registered steamship *Montezuma* berthing at Millwall Dock where the generous dimensions of the lock allowed the largest vessels of the day to enter from the Thames. The postcard was written in 1905 by another local resident, Walter Robinson of 37 Alpha Road.

The frozen Thames 1895. The river in unfamiliar mood with ice floes and packed ice on the shore during the severe winter of 1895. The scene was at Greenwich Reach off the Isle of Dogs where conditions prevented the sailing of the cross-Thames ferries. The photograph was ten years old when revived for this Edwardian postcard.

Crossing the river, Greenwich to Isle of Dogs. This is one of a series of 'then and now' postcards published by photographers Perkins & Son of Lewisham around 1905. The old Isle of Dogs ferry was rendered redundant from 1902 when the Greenwich foot tunnel opened having taken some six years to build. The tunnel was designed by London County Council engineer Alexander Binnie and features distinctive rotundas at either end.

Blackwall Pier and entrance to East India Dock Basin, c. 1905. Located between the Isle of Dogs and the river Lea, Blackwall can boast a lengthy maritime heritage, with ship repairing and building dating from the fifteenth century, and with Blackwall stairs providing the starting point for the Virginia Settlers under John Smith who set sail in 1606 to found the first British colony in North America. The East India Company's docks opened in 1806 handling cargoes of merchandise from the Orient. The view looks eastward towards Leamouth with Orchard and Union Wharves and the twin towers of Thames Ironworks on the skyline. Also visible are a pair of lighthouses on Trinity House Buoy Wharf; one of them still stands as London's only lighthouse.

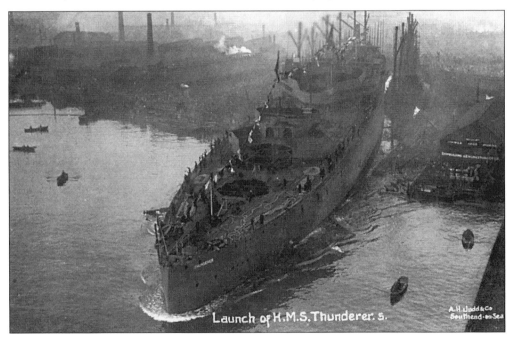

Launch of HMS *Thunderer*, Thames Ironworks & Shipbuilding Co., Bow Creek, 1 February 1911. At 22,000 tons, this was the largest warship to be launched on the Thames, but its construction financially ruined the shipbuilders and the yard, founded in 1846, closed in 1912. Bow Creek is the Thames-side reach of the river Lea.

Meat convoy in Beckton Road, dock strike, June 1912. Strikes have periodically crippled London's docks, and during the early 1900s a variety of scenes associated with the conflicts were pictured on the postcards of the day. This one by G.L. Shotter of Barking Road shows a convoy making its way from the docks to the London markets under police protection to guard against attacks by militant strikers.

Feeding children during the dock strike, 1912. Lengthy dock strikes created food shortages but as may be seen from this rare postcard by Messrs Bird and Thomas of Custom House, efforts were made to ensure that no child went hungry. The postcard was sent by one of the volunteer meal-ladies depicted with a message revealing that nearly 2,000 children were given a noonday meal at this (unnamed) Board school near Victoria Docks.

Three

Stepney, Wapping, Limehouse and Whitechapel

Whitechapel High Street and Commercial Road (Gardiner's Corner), c. 1906. The grand emporium of Gardiner & Company, clothiers and outfitters, made an impressive gateway to the East End from Aldgate and was a mecca for generations of East Enders who found the store a useful amenity. The original shop dated from 1839 when two tailoring Gardiner brothers from Glasgow journeyed London-wards and set up their first outlet in Aldgate under the name The Scotch House. The lofty clock tower of Gardiner's premises looked down on the chaotic traffic junction which eventually took its name, and which lived on after the store was destroyed in a spectacular blaze during May 1972.

John Scholes Ltd, Carmen and Haulage Contractors, Royal Mint Street, *c.* 1925. A publicity postcard for this firm who had additional premises in Walburgh Street, Stepney. These powerful steam-driven wagons gradually began to replace the horses which had previously been used for heavy road haulage.

Cable Street looking west, *c.* 1906. A coloured Fielding postcard showing on the left, St George's Town Hall which was originally the Vestry hall of St George-in-the-East (1860). The bow windows of the neighbouring library are seen with the Britannia pub on the Prospect Place corner. War damage here was severe and the buildings on the right were replaced by Stepney Borough Council's Tarling Estate West housing scheme.

Ratcliff Highway/St George Street (The Highway), *c.* 1906. It was once the principal street of St George-in-the-East but a series of grisly murders in 1811 brought notoriety and a change of name to St George Street. The 1900s saw a partial return to the original name and a change in character as any old buildings spared by the Blitz were swept away. This Fielding postcard shows Harris Libman's tobacco shop, left, the Jolly Sailor pub and the premises of naturalist and wild animals dealer Albert Jamrach whose stock sometimes included exotic creatures brought home from distant lands by returning seamen.

Docker's cottages, Pennington Street by John's Hill, *c.* 1906. The first East Enders to live in these early eighteenth century cottages would have enjoyed a rural outlook towards the Thames but all that changed with the building in 1811 of Tobacco Dock with its awesome perimeter wall.

Old houses, Pennington Street, c. 1930. The houses in the preceding view are seen again but in this later view their number and condition has diminished somewhat. Partial demolition to the right has opened up a view of the backs of equally ancient houses in John's Hill, while to the left another long run of these remarkable survivals stretched towards Breezer's Hill.

Old houses, Pennington Street by Chigwell Hill, c. 1930. The towering walls of a Tobacco Dock warehouse cast a deep shadow along another run of eighteenth century cottages with Old Gravel Lane (Wapping Lane) showing up in the distance. The two postcard views on this page were photographed by an amateur who was obviously attracted by these survivals of old Ratcliff, few of which subsequently withstood the devastation of the Blitz.

Opposite: The Rose & Crown, 203 St George Street (The Highway), c. 1913. Dockers and seafarers pubs abounded hereabouts, this one stood between the long-vanished Ship Alley and Neptune Street, now Wellclose Street. To the left, a wall poster advertises cinema performances at the Royal Cambridge Theatre of Varieties in Commercial Street and is partly written in Yiddish for the benefit of the Jewish people then living in this part of London.

PAULIN'S
FINE
ALES

MANN, CROSSMAN & PAULIN'S LTD
CELEBRATED ALES, IMPERIAL STOUT & PORTER.

The
ROSE &
CROWN

Burton
& PALE
ALE
STORES.

The
ROSE &
CROWN.
Foreign
WINE &
SPIRIT
STORES.

DUNVILLE'S
V R
WHISKY

JOHN
JAMESONS

CAMBRIDGE

CAMBRIDGE
MATINEES

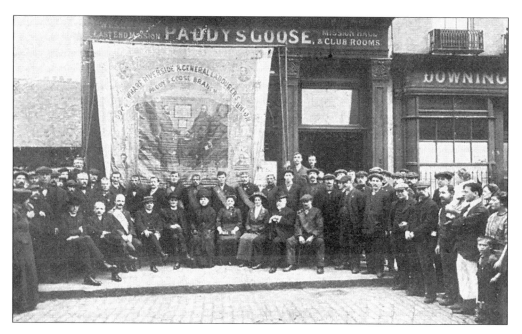

Paddy's Goose Hall, 225, Shadwell High Street, c. 1913. Located in the high street of another of the Tower Hamlets, Shadwell, these premises held meetings of the Wesleyan East End Mission together with the Dock Wharf Riverside & General Labourers Union. In the nineteenth century this was a raucous pub serving a lively clientele of Irish settlers in the East End. The pub was then the White Swan, a bird which attracted the nickname 'Paddy's Goose'.

Calman Greenspan, provisions dealer, 90 Watney Street, Shadwell. Located in the shadow of the Shadwell station railway bridge, the Greenspan family traded from this and other addresses in Watney Street, their shops supplemented by street stalls. This fine postcard photograph catches Calman and Celia Greenspan with their staff and delivery wagon around 1913.

Charles Fielding, tobacconist and stationer, Watney Street, Shadwell, c. 1906. Some of the postcards which illustrate chapters two and three originate from this shop – a selection of them may be seen in the window on the left facing Chapman Street. The postcards were printed in rich colours and a display of them does much to recall the atmosphere of the inner East End of a century ago.

Watney Market, Watney Street, Shadwell, c. 1906. Another Fielding card, this time showing the street market at the Commercial Road end of Watney Street. The rows of domestic stores included at no. 26 another branch of the Greenspan empire with Calman trading here as a cheese-monger. To the right a pair of hanging lamps adorn the Mason's Arms pub beside Blakesley Street. A new Watney Market has arisen on the war damaged site of the old one.

CHRIST CHURCH, WATNEY STREET.

Christ Church, Watney Street, *c.* 1906. Building work on this Norman style church with its twin towers and notable interior began in 1841, but a century later on 16 April 1941 the church lay in ruins following the explosion of a Second World War landmine. This Fielding postcard depicts the church whose site was covered in 1967 by the Watney Market housing estate.

Raine's Foundation School, Cannon Street Road, *c.* 1906. The school was founded in 1719 in the parish of St George-in-the-East by wealthy brewer Henry Raine – it transferred to new premises in Arbour Square in 1913. The school occupied buildings on both sides of Cannon Street Road, the girl's and infants school seen here was on the eastern side and has been demolished but what was once the boy's school can still be seen on the opposite side. This Fielding postcard was posted in 1909 by someone living at no. 20, Shadwell High Street.

RAINES GIRLS SCHOOL, CANNON ST, RD, E

The Spencer Arms, Dean Street, *c.* 1910. Dean Street ran a lengthy course from Cable Street to Commercial Road passing Abraham Nehard's grocery shop, far left, and Silas Hill's beer house on the Spencer Street corner along the way – Mr. Hills, his family and large dog are seen here in their doorway. Stepney Council's Tarling Estate replaced this old neighbourhood soon after the Second World War with Sheridan House marking the site of Dean Street. Sheridan Street also ran close by.

Catholic procession, Commercial Road by Harding Street (Steel's Lane), *c.* 1911. A religious procession braves the rain and gloom of Commercial Road as it passes Morris Rayner's hairdressing saloon on the Harding Street corner and the long-vanished Mechanic's Arms beer house, centre.

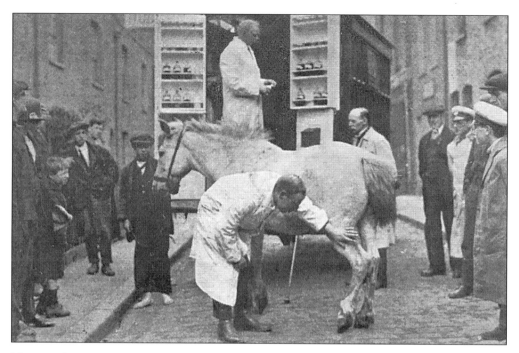

The People's Dispensary for Sick Animals of the Poor, Commercial Road, *c.* 1923. London in the 1920s still relied on a vast population of horses for haulage and other tasks. The animals were often overworked and poorly maintained especially in less affluent areas where horses were still working while in very poor health. Titled 'Not One Sound Foot' this postcard highlights the work of one organization whose mobile dispensary brought relief to suffering animals throughout the East End and elsewhere.

La Corniere Ltd., 83 Mansell Street, Whitechapel, *c.* 1910. The animal seen in the preceding picture might have benefited from this remedy which was 'guaranteed to cure every "affection" of the horse's hoof', which indeed it should have done when priced at a lofty five shillings a jar. This local company's postcard advertisement helped to spread the word.

Commercial Road and Leman Street, (Gardiner's Corner), Whitechapel, *c.* 1928. The complex road and tramway junction at Gardiner's Corner showing the Wheatsheaf pub with its electric 'Bovril' sign. Leman Street is to the right and the traffic island reveals a telephone for the use of inspectors controlling the tram system.

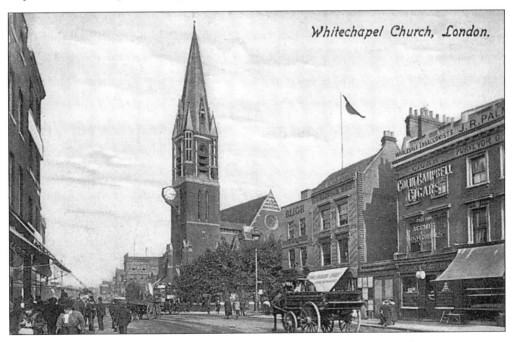

High Street Whitechapel, *c.* 1906. The church of St Mary Matfelon towers skywards on the site of the thirteenth century White Chapel from which the name Whitechapel derives. Dating from 1875, the red-brick building seen here was the last in a long sequence of churches – it was destroyed in the Blitz. A postcard by Messrs Roberts of Mile End Road.

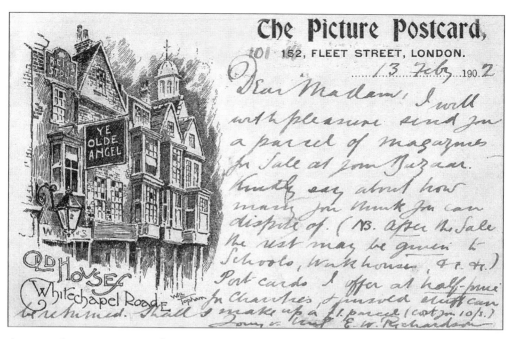

A postcard magazine postcard, 1900. By 1900 increasingly attractive postcards were appearing in quantity and enticing many people into a new collecting craze. With it came the *Picture Postcard & Collector's Chronicle*, the first British magazine devoted to the burgeoning hobby. The magazine was accompanied by a series of publicity cards, one of which featured this charming sketch of Ye Old Angel Inn on Whitechapel High Street, part of an ancient row which would be replaced by a new 'Old Angel' and Whitechapel Art Gallery in 1901. Messages were written on the picture side of the earliest postcards.

Whitechapel Road, *c.* 1905. A long-vanished section of Whitechapel Road with its mixture of Jewish businesses, pubs and tiny side turnings. Of these, Size Yard has gone but still extant Kings Arms Court recalls an old inn. To the left was Jacobs & Bresloff's shoe shop with the Jewish Colonial Bank next door.

48

Sidney Street Siege, 3 January 1911. During the first decades of the twentieth century, postcard photographers sometimes found themselves in the role of photo-journalists picturing local and national events, the postcards finding a ready market in that era of sparsely illustrated newspapers - Sidney Street's legendary siege was a notable example. The story began when a pair of armed Russian anarchists murdered three policemen following a failed attempt to rob a jeweller's shop in Houndsditch. The pair fled to a house in Sidney Street where for seven hours they resisted the efforts of the police and a detachment of Scots Guards to apprehend them.

Sidney Street Siege. When the anarchists fired on the authorities, the fire was returned and a ferocious gun battle ensued with the situation becoming serious enough for the Home Secretary, Winston Churchill, to attend and direct operations. Eventually fire broke out in the anarchist's house, quickly consuming the entire building complete with the fugitives for whom there was no escape. These postcards were typical of dozens produced to record this dramatic day in the East End.

Sidney Street Siege. The anarchist's house on fire as portrayed on an East London Printing Co. postcard. The card's message records the thoughts of someone who had just visited this Jewish quarter of the East End: 'I have just been over the battlefield where this postcard was purchased from a very pleasant looking Jew. Up here it is all Houndsditch and Sidney Street – we hear nothing else. Almost everyone I passed was gabbling over something in Yiddish'.

Sidney Street Seige, the British Queen pub, Cannon Street Road by Salter Street. Although police cordons kept the public at a fairly safe distance stray bullets inflicted a number of minor injuries. One victim was a Mr Berman who was struck on the head, but his discomfiture was somewhat relieved by Harry Barker, landlord of the British Queen with a glass of 'Mann, Crossman & Paulin's Celebrated Ale'. The brewery was not slow to capitalise upon this morsel of publicity with a souvenir postcard.

Pavilion Theatre, Whitechapel Road near Vallance Road, *c.* 1908. This landmark of the Jewish East End first opened its doors in November 1828 when it was also known as the Eastern Opera House. The theatre burnt down in 1856, and was rebuilt in 1865 with reconstruction following in 1874 and 1894. As the local Jewish population increased through the 1800s, the Pavilion staged Yiddish plays, cantorial concerts and was used as a synagogue on High Holy days. Later years brought boxing and wrestling promotions. The postcard was 'phototyped in France' and shows the theatre with its Yiddish posters and neighbouring premises including the Pavilion Refreshment Rooms and Josiah Zimelman's jewellery shop. The road works mark the construction of the electric tramway.

Royal Visit, Whitechapel Bell Foundry, 1919. A proud day in the long history of Whitechapel Bell Foundry when two bells for Westminster Abbey were cast in the presence of King George V, Queen Mary and Princess Mary, while outside crowds jammed Whitechapel Road in the hope of a glimpse of Their Majesties. Whitechapel Bell Foundry is London's oldest business having begun in Houndsditch in 1420 – it has cast some of the world's most famous bells including Big Ben and America's Liberty Bell. Postcards of royal visits have always enjoyed great popularity.

The Salvation Army's Food and Shelter Depot and City Colony Headquarters, 20-22 Whitechapel Road, c. 1910. The building is adorned by a poster portrait of General William F Booth who created the Salvation Army in 1878. The postcard is from a series which features the work of the Salvation Army in poorer parts of London.

London Hospital (The Royal London Hospital), Whitechapel Road, c. 1904. The hospital was founded in Moorfields in 1740, then moved to Prescott Street and in 1753 to its present site. When Queen Victoria opened a new wing in 1876, it became the largest hospital in the country. The gabled facade seen here was added in 1890 and further building added to the hospital through the twentieth century. The Queen visited in July 1990 for the hospital's 250th anniversary. The postcard by John Walker in the Bells series shows a typically busy Whitechapel Road with a Borough of Stepney water cart laying the dust of an Edwardian summer.

London Hospital, c. 1917. An anonymously produced postcard of wounded 'tommies' (soldiers) being cared for during the First World War. Postcards were at the height of their popularity during this period of conflict.

Stepney Esperanto Group at Alexandra Palace, *c.* 1907. Picture postcards were produced for many kinds of minority groups including this one for Stepney's devotees of Esperanto, an artificial language created in 1880 by Dr Louis Zamenhof of Warsaw. The card was sent by local Esperantist H.A. Epstein of Hare Street, Bethnal Green, and naturally enough the message is written in Esperanto.

Spring Gardens Place (Stepney Way), *c.* 1910. The ancient village of Stepney with St Dunstan's, centre, the mother church of the East End. It has been here since Saxon times but the old neighbourhood has gone including the Old Green Dragon pub by Grosvenor Street and the shops by Old Church Road, right. Stepping Stones urban farm is now on the left.

Mile End & Stepney Cripples Parlour, John Pound's Mission, Oxford Street (Stepney Way), c. 1908. The John Pound Mission was prominent among London centres in developing educational and social work among crippled children. The mission held weekly meetings, one of which is seen here, where the children could enjoy games, scrapbooks and postcard albums. The mission held an annual tea which in 1908 was attended by the Mayor of Stepney.

East End street life. Although the place and date are unknown (it looks like the 1930s), this amateur photographer's snapshot printed in postcard form gives a wonderful impression of a happy childhood moment in an old East End street.

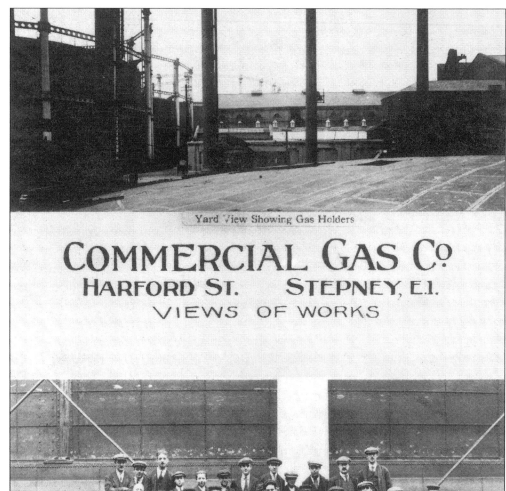

Yard View Showing Gas Holders

COMMERCIAL GAS Cº

HARFORD ST.   STEPNEY, E.1.

VIEWS OF WORKS

The Commercial Gas Co., Stepney Gasworks, Harford Street, c. 1920. An historic site for the production of gas in the East End, the Commercial Gas Light & Coke Co. built their works from 1838, the site still retaining gas-holders dating from 1853. There was a new name, the Commercial Gas company from 1847 and by the 1870s they were supplying gas to much of the inner East End. In the heyday of the picture postcard, even unglamorous places like gas works and power stations were pictured.

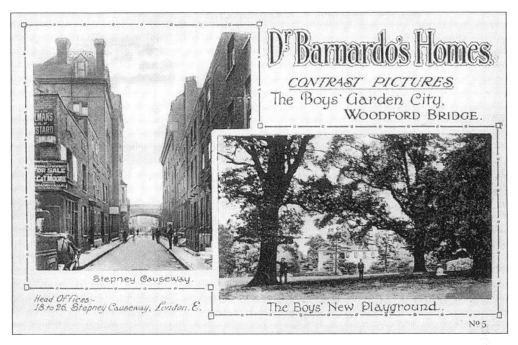

Dr Barnardo's Homes, c. 1910. Numerous postcards have been produced which celebrate the life, work and ultimately the death of one of the most revered of all East Enders, Dublin born Thomas Barnardo. who came to the London Hospital as a student in 1866. Deeply moved by the plight of the East End's multitude of homeless children, Thomas Barnardo devoted his life to their protection, advancement and education and opened a first lodging house for them in Stepney Causeway in 1870. Dr Barnardo went on to create a network of children's homes, his work continuing after his death in 1905. The postcard highlights the contrast between old Stepney Causeway and a newly opened 'Boy's Garden City' at Woodford, Essex.

Barnardo Boys learning a craft at the wheelwright's shop in Stepney Causeway, c. 1908.

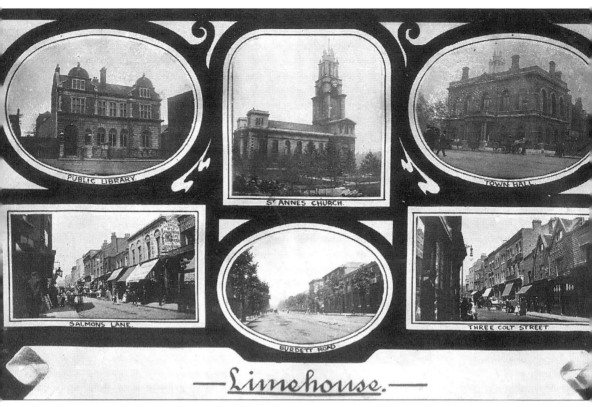

—*Limehouse*.—

Limehouse, *c.* 1906. Multiple view postcards have enjoyed popular appeal from the earliest days when continental examples were based on paintings and engravings – multiple views based on photographs were an onward development from around 1897. This example highlights the delights of Limehouse and was a good specimen of its type – sometimes a card like this would display the entire output of a more localised photographer; unfortunately this one has remained anonymous. The views working clockwise from the top left are: the Passmore Edwards Public Library, Commercial Road – the foundation stone was laid by J.Passmore Edwards on 19 October 1900. Centre top: St Anne's church, Commercial Road, the grand creation of Nicholas Hawksmoot, one of his trio of mighty East End churches and the parish church of Limehouse. Building began in 1714 but following fire damage in 1850 it was rebuilt by local architect John Morris together with Philip Hardwick. The church tower clock was once the highest in London.

Top right: Limehouse Town Hall which dates from 1879. Lower right: Three Colt Street, an ancient thoroughfare which took its name from an old inn. Three Colt Street is now a road of municipal flats but the view gives a reminder of its earlier incarnation with shops lining the road and a range of historic weatherboarded properties which survived into the twentieth century – they stood opposite Ropemakers Fields whose name is a reminder of an industry which once flourished here. Lower centre: Burdett Road, a purpose built highway dating from 1862 to link the docks with the east/west road route at Mile End. Lower left: Salmon Lane, a once rural byway which led to St Anne's church, hence its original name, Sermon Lane. It now typifies modern Limehouse with its profusion of flats but a century ago there was a bustling street market complemented by shops and pubs. Abraham Woolfson's tobacco shop can be spotted with Frank Ragett's beer shop marked by an extravagant lamp.

Bekesbourne Buildings, Bekesbourne Street, Limehouse, c. 1925. Bekesbourne Buildings was a block of 73 flats built by the London County Council before the First World War. The flats gave their occupants vastly superior housing to the cramped Victorian terraces more usual here - the gardens gave a welcome touch of greenery.

Dundee Wharf, Three Colt Street, Limehouse, c. 1908. While much of old maritime Limehouse has been swept away, these buildings with their tiny cupola and weathervane still stand, the gates to the left leading now to a large complex of apartments which perpetuate the name of Dundee Wharf. In former times it was possible to voyage from here to Dundee and other Scottish ports on one of the steam ships of the Dundee, Perth & London Shipping Co. A time worn postcard of unknown origin.

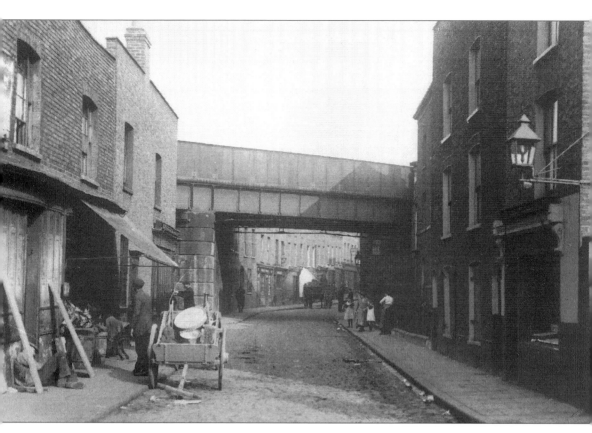

Limehouse Causeway by Salter Street and Trinidad Street, *c.* 1908. This was part of London's original 'Chinatown', one of the capital's more exotic ethnic communities which developed in the nineteenth century as seamen from a variety of east Asian countries, the employees of shipping companies using the local docks, settled and raised families in this corner of the East End. The Chinese people were centred in the narrow streets and alleys around Limehouse Causeway and Pennyfields where all things Chinese were procurable and tightly shuttered shop-fronts were likely to conceal a shadowy opium smoking room or gambling parlour. It was in Limehouse's Chinatown that many Londoners were first introduced to the delights of oriental cuisine with some of the capital's first Chinese, Burmese and Malayan restaurants located hereabouts. The area was never wholly Chinese, however, the last visible shop beyond the bridge in the picture being that of long-established ironmongers John L. Holmes & Son.

   This unknown photographer's postcard captures something of the spirit of old Limehouse and its somewhat dilapidated street-scape before it was all swept away by Stepney Borough Council in the 1930s, the only point of reference now being the railway bridge and viaduct from where the steam trains of the London & Blackwall Railway once enveloped the houses in smoke and sooty smuts. Today the modern Docklands Light Railway uses the viaduct and the bridge houses the system's West Ferry station, while West India Dock Road and West Ferry Road extensions have taken the sites of the shops in the distance. There is nothing today to recall the true antiquity of Limehouse Causeway; it originated around the fifteenth century as a raised road or causeway through the Thames-side marshlands.

Limehouse Causeway looking towards West India Dock Road, c. 1935. A later view of the now non-existent section of Limehouse Causeway with its oriental shops including, centre right, Chong Chu's Refreshment Rooms, an old established Chinese restaurant, and at the far right, Chung King's drapery shop. The whitewashed entrance to tiny Holker Place can be seen between them. Further along was the Britannia Cafe de Anglo Ceylon with a cuisine from the country now called Sri Lanka.

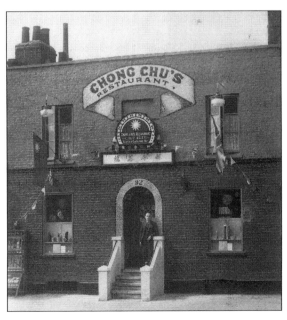

Chong Chu's Restaurant, 92 West India Dock Road, c. 1940. Restaurateur Chong Chu stands at the door of his newly opened premises soon after leaving his original abode in Limehouse Causeway. Chong Chu has written a bilingual 'good luck' greeting on this card. His premises were once those of the Chinese Mission House which was run by Revd George Piercy who, having spent thirty years in China was highly respected by the East End's Chinese community.

The site of the Catholic church of Our Lady Immaculate, Commercial Road by Island Row and Norway Place, c. 1904. The church originated as a mission, begun in 1881 for the local Irish population, but under the guidance of the inspirational Father Higley (rector from 1888 to 1934), a building fund was set up to provide a new church. As part of his campaign, Father Higley posted quantities of these cards with the message 'I want to build a church in this poor place worthy of Our Lady Immaculate. Will you help me with a shilling' – this example was sent to the English College in Rome. Father Higley's new church was begun in 1926 and finished in 1934.

The Old Nautical House, Commercial Road by Three Colt Street. Limehouse, c. 1905. A useful port of call for the homecoming seaman, this was a pawnbroker's shop where a trinket acquired in a foreign land could be turned into ready cash as the pub beckoned. Nautical instruments, including sextants, chronometers and telescopes abounded in an emporium founded in 1810 by a Mr Dicker before Robert George acquired the business.

Opposite: Pennyfields, Limehouse, c. 1935. It looks like a typical East End street but this too was a road at the centre of Limehouse's old Chinese community. The view looks eastwards towards Turner's Buildings and the Silver Lion pub with the projecting sign of the Three Tuns seen along the way. Eva Lowing's chandlers shop is on the left. Pennyfields eventually crumbled into dereliction and flats arose in the 1950s and 1960s.

The Cape of Good Hope, Commercial Road, Limehouse, c. 1906. Many of the street, place and pub names in the old seafaring communities of the East End recall far away places and have a rather nautical flavour. The Cape of Good Hope was one example and the wording 'Captains and Shippers supplied' above the entrance welcomed the home-coming seaman. An 1880 rebuilding of an earlier inn, the pub stood by St Anne Street whose tiny houses can be seen on this photographic postcard. Modern Cape House marks the site.

The Edinburgh Castle, Rhodeswell Road, Limehouse, c. 1908. This former pub and music hall was acquired by Thomas Barnardo and was opened as a working men's club and people's mission church in 1873, although it retained its splendidly castellated pub exterior. Part of Mile End Stadium was built on the site in 1952.

Four

Poplar and the
Isle of Dogs

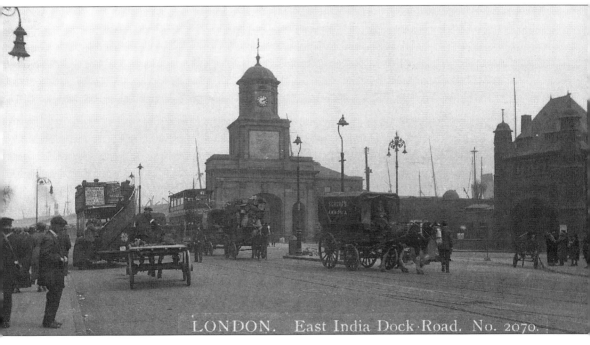

LONDON. East India Dock·Road. No. 2070.

East India Dock Road, c. 1925. Poplar is one of the three former Metropolitan Boroughs which today make up the modern London Borough of Tower Hamlets. Its transformation from a village in the Middlesex countryside to an integral part of maritime and industrial London was mostly achieved early in the nineteenth century as major dockland construction changed the long Thames frontage for ever. The southernmost part of Poplar is the urban peninsula of the Isle of Dogs which, with the river on three sides made an ideal locality for dock building. The creation of the West India Docks in 1801 across the neck of the peninsula surrounded it with water – it was now an island in more than just name. The decline of the docks from the 1960s left a blighted landscape but a great plan of regeneration from the 1980s has seen the mighty towers of Canary Wharf rising above an Island reborn as one of the capital's most vibrant areas. The postcard is of East India Dock Road, a highway begun in 1806 as an extension of Commercial Road and to take heavy dockland traffic away from narrow High Street Poplar. The entrances to East India Docks (1805, rebuilt 1913),and Blackwall Tunnel (1891-7) are seen, both buildings having perished in the interests of modern traffic flow. Another of the animated Degen/Lewis postcards.

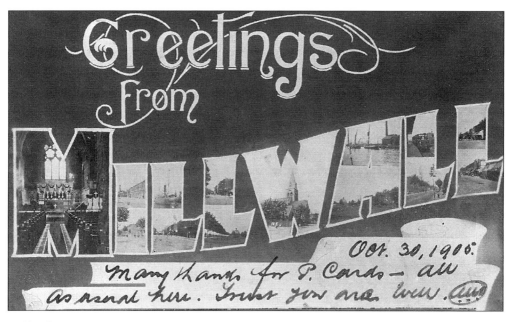

Millwall views, c. 1905. Millwall is in the western part of the Isle of Dogs and was noted for its shipbuilders and other riverside industries. The tiny pictures seen within the Millwall name include St Luke's church, Strafford Street, built in 1868 and demolished in 1960 following war damage. Also recognisable are Millwall Dock, Island Gardens, and Millwall Extension Railway with East and West Ferry Roads.

Millwall view, c. 1905. Multiple view cards were popular in Millwall, this selection includes Pier Head Cottages, the Millwall Omnibus, High Bridge, Millwall Dock and St Paul's Presbyterian church which was built for Scottish labourers who worked for Millwall shipbuilders. The building is now used for theatre and is called The Space. Other pictures are of the Isle of Dogs Fire Station (1904) and the congregational church.

West Ferry Road by Tooke Street, *c.* 1905. The shops and houses faced the landward side of Millwall's docks and wharves in an area once known as Tooke Town, named after a local landowner. Large signs on the Tooke Street corner point the way to James Rattray's Islander's pub at no. 3 Tooke Street, while coster's barrows added to the shopper's choice along the main road. The Barkantine Estate arose from 1965-70 on the site of old Tooke Town and the Quarterdeck shopping parades have replaced the old facilities.

West Ferry Road, *c.* 1905. West Ferry Road was built in 1812 as the Deptford and Greenwich Road – it led to the cross-Thames ferry at the southern tip of the Island. The view here is of the houses and shops by Maria and Malabar Streets – a far from peaceful place for those living here with the iron-shod wheels of heavy commercial wagons crashing over the road surfacing of granite setts. The shape of these locally produced cards is most unusual.

Malabar Street from West Ferry Road, *c.* 1906. The old houses have gone as has the Salvation Army Hall behind its lamp, right, but part of the street itself still exists beyond Cheval Street, centre. The scene is now dominated by the twenty-one storied Midship Point, a tower of flats, part of the Barkantine Estate.

Millwall Football Club, 1905-6 season. The Island's professional football team is thought to have sprung from a team of players who worked at Morton's food processing factory West Ferry Road in 1885. The club moved to 'The Den', New Cross, in 1910 but is pictured here while still playing on the Island at what is now Millwall Park. The postcard by a Mr Pycock of Upper North Street, Poplar, was sent to one of his neighbours with the message 'This is a photo of the bonny blue of Millwall'.

East Ferry Road by Glengall Road, Isle of Dogs, *c.* 1906. The writer of this postcard points out 'our village post office', the East Ferry Road Branch Office which shared premises with tailor George Parrett and served a population of workers, dockers and their families. The inner man was well catered for next door at the Anchor Dining Rooms which was also a 'good pull-up for car men' with water available for their horses. Glengall Road, left, led to Millwall Dock Station (now Crossharbour). The Docklands Arena is now a major attraction in this regenerated area.

The George, Glengall Road by East Ferry Road, *c.* 1906. This postcard was sent by Mr and Mrs Evers of Glengall Road for whom this vast Victorian pub was their 'local' – rebuilding would reduce the size of the George in later years. Its locality was once the scene of the daily ritual of the 'call-on' where stevedores gathered to seek a days work – the George would then open at 6 a.m. to serve coffee and rum.

Manchester Road by Stebondale Street, Cubitt Town, c. 1925. Development of the south-eastern corner of the Isle of Dogs was begun in 1842 by William Cubitt who created an area of riverside industry and streets of houses for the workers. They called it Cubitt Town after its creator, but following the Blitz little remains of the original concept other than the landmark Christ Church. The postcard gives a reminder of the distinctive Cubitt terraces and the shops which served the community including that of provisions dealer F.H. Benwell on the Stebondale Street corner. The post-war housing of Clipper House on the Schooner Estate is here now.

Manchester Road by Parsonage Street, c. 1910. Cubitt Town was spaciously laid out with plentiful greenery, and the later houses to be built featured bay windows and basements. The postcard was sent by a resident of Billson Street.

The London Tavern, Manchester Road by Glengall Road, 1941. It is 1941 and the desolation of wartime London is all too evident in this image showing what remained of a once busy Cubitt Town pub. A variety of stark wartime posters cling to the walls offering advice for those bombed out of their homes, while one from the Ministry of Food informs housewives of the Poplar Food Campaign with its 'Wartime Cookery Demonstrations'. Glengall Road, left, once crossed almost the full width of the Island.

The Fire station, East India Dock Road, c. 1905. Fire stations and their activities were popular postcard subjects – this example was one of London County Council's older stations. The heavy polluting industry of this locality is glimpsed in the background with Thomas Moy, coal merchant, left, and further back, a company which supplied clinker, slag and hardcore.

East India Dock Road by Stainsby Street (now Canton Street), *c.* 1907. The Stainsby pub occupied one Stainsby Street corner while the Princes Theatre (soon to become the Poplar Hippodrome) graced the further one. The theatre opened on Boxing Day, 1905, and is seen here when part of its entertainment included the showing of 'animated pictures', predating the arrival of Poplar's first purpose-built cinema. The Fulham-bound motor bus has no route number as was usual in 1907.

East India Dock Road by Ann Street, *c.* 1909. John Willis' newspaper shop stood on the Ann Street corner, right, while next door locals could enjoy themselves at George Christey's Automatic Exhibition with its slot machines and automata. Further along, the Tramway Tobacco Store's name celebrated the then new electric transport system. The Sir John Franklin pub is in the centre of the view, this marking the point by St Leonard's Road up to which the shops have gone in favour of a vast road scheme, the Blackwall Tunnel Approach.

St Leonard's Road from East India Dock Road, *c.* 1904. The Sir John Franklin pub takes the East India Dock Road corner, left, while beyond, the tiny shops stretch away into Poplar's hinterland. The sites of everything on the right have been taken for the Blackwall Tunnel Approach – the locally made postcard revealing this lost neighbourhood of shops, pubs and side streets which included Albert, Bloomsbury and Rowlett Streets.

St Leonard's Road by Burcham Street, *c.* 1905. Here too, the small shops and homes of old Poplar have given way to post-war housing, the shop of grocer Henry Smith having long since departed the Burcham Street corner, left. The church of St Michael & All Angels is still a focal point, albeit in a new role as St Michael's Court, a residential conversion.

Chrisp Street, looking South, Poplar.

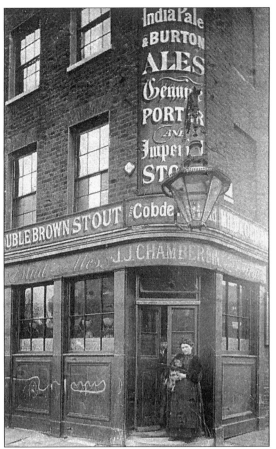

Chrisp Street looking towards East India Dock Road, *c.* 1910. This coloured postcard was sent to Guernsey, the sender describing the street as 'half a mile both sides of the road, stalls crowded every evening, Saturday especially'. The photographer has caught a good crowd of East Enders thronging the market and its shops including those of Bernard Sporing, watchmaker, left, and Harry Neaves, house-furnisher, right, both of whom occupied corners of Grundy Street. In 1951, a new market place replaced the old war-damaged facilities.

The Cobden Head, St Leonard's Road by Cobden Street, *c.* 1905. John Chamberlin's beer shop was a modest affair when compared with the opulent gin-palaces of Victorian and Edwardian London, but the fine lamp would have shone out brightly to welcome the clientele. The graffiti of the day, left, was in easily removable chalk. (Maurice Friedman Collection).

Broomfield Street and Guildford Road (Godalming Road) from Upper North Street, Poplar, c. 1919. With a brass band at its head, the annual Catholic Parade makes its way along Broomfield Street towards Upper North Street. These parades were a considerable spectacle and attracted crowds of onlookers. Guildford Road became Godalming Road in the 1930s but was built over in post-war years.

Augusta Street, Poplar, 1919. Augusta Street celebrates the victory which ended the First World War with a traditional East End street party and colourful patriotic decorations. Similar jubilations followed the Second World War but by then the postcard craze was over and cards were rarely made. Both postcards on this page were the work of photographer Thomas Mace of Kerbey Street.

Grundy Street (now Brownfield Street), by Nye Street, c. 1905. Modern housing has replaced this section of Grundy Street where the City Mission Hall stood on the Nye Street corner. On the further corner, fading lettering points the way to a cow-keeper's premises; 'The Public may go into the cow house and have the milk direct from the cow. Milking hours from 6 to 8 a.m.' Before 1906 milk was supplied in jugs rather than bottles.

Fire at Cotton Street Baptist Chapel, 23 May 1914. Postcard views of fires and other local disasters were popular at a time when such images rarely appeared in any other form. The unknown photographer who captured this scene also caught the London Fire Brigade in action and police holding back the onlookers. Cotton Street now channels traffic to and from Canary Wharf and the Isle of Dogs.

Five
Spitalfields, Eastern Shoreditch and Bethnal Green

Spitalfield Market, Commercial Street, *c.* 1905. A century ago, Spitalfields lay at the centre of a vast area of London markets which sold everything from garments and household goods at Petticoat Lane, to bicycles, dogs and caged birds at Brick Lane and Club Row. Spitalfields itself housed London's wholesale fruit and vegetable market, an institution founded in 1682 on the site of the twelfth century priory and hospital of St Mary Spital while Roman remains discovered near the market point to Spitalfields' true antiquity. The early eighteenth century brought Huguenot silk weavers and merchants to the fine houses then being built on the Spital Fields, followed by Jewish immigrants in the nineteenth century with more recent arrivals from Bangladesh all adding to the areas colourful appeal. The postcard was written by a Spitalfields dealer who complains that 'trade has been bad'.

Spital Square from White Lion Street (now Folgate Street), *c.* 1905. Spitalfields is noted for its Georgian houses, the grandest of which were the merchant's houses in Spital Square, but continued expansion of the market has left few reminders of them there. No. 15, right, was demolished in 1952 but has been recreated in replica to restore some of the historic townscape. The postcard by the City Studios of Bishopsgate Without also shows the Poltava or German Synagogue whose congregation moved here from New Broad Street in 1884. The synagogue and adjoining houses were replaced by a fruit warehouse in the 1930s.

Christ Church Spitalfields National School, *c.* 1907. Young East Enders pose for their class photograph outside the school which stands in Brick Lane between Fashion and Fournier Streets. The school moved to Brick Lane in 1873 having previously stood in the churchyard of Christ Church which dates from 1714.

SAVING THE RUINS

Spital Yard, Spital Square, *c*. 1908. Another postcard from the City Studios, this one showing building work in progress in this tiny cul-de-sac which leads out of the southern arm of Spital Square. The City of London boundary passes through Spital Yard where a commemorative plaque marks the birthplace of Susanna Annesley, mother of John Wesley, the founder of Methodism, The background buildings, which included the City Toilet Club, a hairdressers at No. 1 Spital Square, were demolished in 1929 for road widening.

Fashion Street Arcade, the Moorish Market, 1905. Middle Eastern exotica in Spitalfields with this splendid Moorish folly which ran almost the full length of Fashion Street. It was built in 1905 and contained 63 shops but innovative architecture is not always a recipe for commercial success – the venture failed and in 1909 the lessee was ejected for non payment of rent. The building proved more durable however, and much of it still stands. This postcard was issued for the opening of the arcade.

The George & Guy, Brick Lane by Fashion Street, c. 1911. George Willers was landlord of this prominent pub, which sported a fine pair of lamps and offered a bottle of gin for 2/6d and a glass of Wincarnis for 2d. The pub closed long ago but the building survives.

Sclater Street bird market, *c*. 1910. Eighteenth century Huguenot settlers popularised the keeping of caged birds in the East End, and it was to Sclater Street's bird dealers that generations of Londoners flocked to acquire a new feathered friend. The postcard from the Rotary Photographic series shows the cages hanging outside the shops with Brick Lane in the distance and the suitably ornithologically named Cygnet Street on the left.

Sclater Street bird market from Brick Lane, *c*. 1908. Another view of this highly individual trading place taken from a series of postcards which feature London's street markets. The building on the Brick Lane corner, right, still stands complete with its eighteenth century street name plaque.

Brick Lane by Sclater Street and Hare Street (Cheshire Street), *c.* 1908. Sunday markets continue to thrive in the cultural melting pot of Brick Lane - this busy scene from nearly a century ago has many similarities to that of today. The Jewish beigel shops are still here and have been joined by the colourful premises of the Bangladeshi community.

The Dog Market, Club Row, Bethnal Green Road, *c.* 1908. This gathering of animal dealers and their stock, (among which fighting was not unknown) combined to create London's noisiest street market. Among the delights on offer here were live rats which were used as bait during dog-fighting contests – once a popular 'sport'. There was also a bicycle market in Club Row.

King Edward Street from Hanbury Street, 1910. An area to the east of Brick Lane was developed from the late seventeenth century as Mile End New Town, but by Victorian times it had degenerated into an overcrowded quarter with small houses, tenements and workshops jostling for what little space there was. King Edward Street typified the district, as seen here with St Olave's church on the right and the premises of East London Carriage & Motor Works on the left. Further along was tiny Meggs Place with its corner shop; the King Edward Ragged School and Old Montague Street in the distance.

St Olave's church, Hanbury Street from King Edward Street, 1910. A youthful group, probably from the Ragged School, gathers by St Olave' s, a Victorian church which stood until around 1914. King Edward Street was renamed Kingward Street in 1939, but it disappeared with the building of the Chicksand Estate, the name living on in Kingward House which now covers the site.

King Edward Street from Old Montague Street, 1910. A third postcard in this sequence by an amateur photographer whose work captures much of the atmosphere of this old East End neighbourhood. Here the view looks along the residential terrace on the right to tiny side-turning Spring Gardens and the Ragged School on the Eele Street corner. The Enterprise pub can be spotted by Chicksand Street with Deal Street School whose building still stands in distant Hanbury Street. The towering premises of Martineau's Brewers Sugar Co. are on the left.

Norton Folgate, *c.* 1904. Once part of Roman Ermine Street, Norton Folgate links Shoreditch High Street with Bishopsgate Without which was so called because it was outside the City wall. The unremarkable premises including a pair of pubs ran up to Worship Street but it is all in marked contrast to the scene here today where the City's mighty Broadgate fills the site.

Norton Folgate, *c.* 1908. The Spitalfields side of Norton Folgate, right, was distinguished by an eighteenth century chemist's shop with a fine double bow- windowed shop-front surmounted by a stone eagle. White Lion Street (Folgate Street from the 1930s) can be seen with Hope Bros hosiers, on the corner. Another card by City Studios (Shadow Catchers).

The Boundary Estate: Iffley, Clifton and Laleham Buildings, *c.* 1905. One of London's most notorious Victorian slums was located close to the boundaries of Spitalfields, Shoredith and Bethnal Green. It was the 'Old Nichol', so named from one of its principal streets, a place whose crime, poverty and horrific living conditions were immortalised in Arthur Morrison's novel *A Child of the Jago* (1896) – the 'Old Jago' in the story being the 'Old Nichol' in all but name. The end of the nineteenth century brought vast changes and in one of its first great municipal housing schemes, the new London County Council set about clearing the slums and creating a new neighbourhood composed of groups of red-brick blocks of flats and new streets radiating out from Arnold Circus, an elevated circular garden on a mound built from the rubble of the old houses. They called it the Boundary Estate but at first the new flats were an unaffordable luxury for many of the East Enders displaced by the clearances. The design of the Boundary Estate was widely admired and was repeated by the LCC elsewhere in London – it also served as a role model for housing schemes outside the capital. The individual blocks were named after places in the Thames Valley, the old suffix 'Buildings' later being dropped in favour of 'House'. A century on, the estate stands largely intact but awaiting a much needed refurbishment.

The postcard preserves an animated scene from Edwardian days on the estate, with children gathering round the photographer in time honoured fashion. It is another in the delightfully named 'Shadow Catchers' series whose cameramen often ventured into areas ignored by other postcard publishers. Being justifiably proud of their new estates, the LCC also issued a set of postcards picturing them – the Council used these for correspondence with its tenants.

Shoreditch High Street from Fairchild Street, c. 1912. Prominently shown here is the Olympia, a music hall whose long theatrical tradition stretched back to 1837 when it was the Royal Standard public house and pleasure gardens. Following several rebuildings and re-namings, it became a cinema in 1926 called the New Olympia Picturedrome. The George pub is seen on Fairchild Street corner, left, with part of Bethnal Green Road on the right.

Shoreditch High Street, c. 1906. This historic street, once part of Roman Ermine Street, winds its way northwards passing another popular East End music hall and theatre, the Shoreditch Empire. This dated from 1856 and had a variety of names including London Music Hall and London Theatre of Varieties – it closed in 1934. To the right, A. Stedall's Costume Warehouse had a rather modernistic look for this early date.

R. & J. Hill, tobacco manufacturers, 175 Shoreditch High Street, c. 1908. Industrial properties were mixed with the shops and pubs of Shoreditch High Street, including these extensive workshops which extended into New Inn Yard and Anning Street at the back. These ladies are seen hand-rolling and packing cigars in the richly aromatic environment associated with such products. The postcard is part of a set distributed by R. & J. Hill to promote the company.

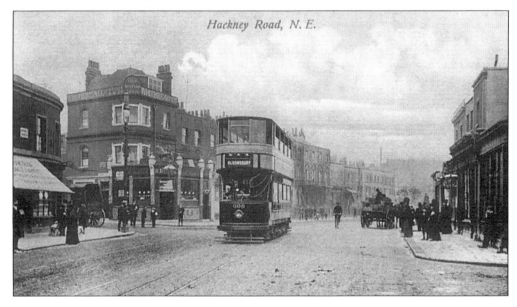

Hackney Road by Weymouth Terrace, c. 1908. Hackney Road ran along the northern boundary of Bethnal Green and was noted for its furniture makers and leather goods dealers, many of whom are still here. The British Lion pub is seen on the Weymouth Terrace corner and the Bloomsbury-bound tram was part of a new fleet of electric cars which had just replaced the old horse-trams.

The North Eastern Hospital for Children (Queen Elizabeth Hospital for Children), Hackney Road, Bethnal Green, c. 1907. The hospital dates from 1867 and was rebuilt and enlarged in 1872 and 1903. When pictured on this Charles Martin postcard, it contained 130 beds and had 74,000 out-patient attendances annually.

The North Eastern Hospital for Children c. 1907. Featuring the children's rooftop playground, this is one of many fund raising postcards issued by the hospital over several decades – sponsored cots were a particular theme of the appeals. In 1968, the hospital came under the control of London's renowned Hospital for Sick Children, Great Ormond Street.

Gibraltar Walk, *c.* 1906. Gibraltar Walk ran from Bethnal Green Road to Virginia Road and featured this attractive group of shops at its northern end. Three lady shop-keepers traded here: Mrs Louisa Barker, haberdasher, Mrs Sarah Lloyd, wardrobe dealer, and Mrs Ellen Lindsay, shirt and collar dresser with Henry Gould, house agent in their midst. The Old Virginia Planter pub and Virginia Road are at the far right.

York Street, Hackney Road, *c.* 1910. With its flat-fronted houses, this was a typical East End street complete with tiny local shops. The little provisions store on the left did not even have a shop window – trading was carried out in the front room. Further along beyond Busk Street was the tiniest of pubs, the Duke of York, located in a single cottage at no. 24.

Bethnal Green Road, by Pollard Row, c. 1907. There was still some agricultural land along Bethnal Green Road at the beginning of the 1800s, but by the century's end it had long gone, and a tightly packed network of streets ran all the way to what was once the village green of old Bethnal Green at Cambridge Road. This Charles Martin postcard gives a good impression of the lively street market with the church of St James the Great in the background. This was built in 1844 of red bricks – it therefore became known as 'The Red Church' but it has since been converted into flats.

Bethnal Green Road looking west, c. 1907. 'The Red Church' appears again beyond a typical row of East End shops and the grander premises of B. Hine, dyers and cleaners. Another of Charles Martin's fine series of East End postcards.

Bethnal Green Road by Hague Street, *c.* 1930. In this later postcard view the scene can still be recognized but the sparse traffic is a less familiar aspect.

Bethnal Green Road by Wilmot Street, c. 1930. Everything looks rather gloomy here – more senior East Enders may remember these murky days when the air was thick with coal smoke before the Clean Air Act dowsed the city's polluting chimneys. The spire rising above the Camden's Head pub, right, belonged to Pott Street Congregational church but this adornment has long gone and the church is now a United Reformed.

Salmon & Ball, Cambridge Road, Bethnal Green. E.

The Salmon & Ball pub, Cambridge Road (Cambridge Heath Road) by Bethnal Green Road, c. 1907. This was a Victorian rebuilding of an inn dating from the 1730s – it briefly held a music hall license in the 1850s. The cameraman had his back to Bethnal Green Gardens which were laid out on the former village green.

The postcard sometimes rather cruelly exploited the physical appearance of a small percentage of the population – this one was a typical example. The young lady was nine-year-old Elizabeth Daltrey, who weighed ten stone and was promoted as 'The Fat and Strong Girl of Bethnal Green' by the makers of Dr Ridge's Food. The back of the card, which dates from around 1910, extols the nutritional values of the product and gives details of Elizabeth's proportions.

Globe Road from Green Street (Roman Road), *c.* 1907. Dramatic changes lay ahead for this, the principal road in Bethnal Green's Globe Town, with multi-storied flats replacing the Rising Sun pub, left, and residential blocks rising on the sites of the little shops and cottages, right.

Fire Station, Green Street (Roman Road) from Globe Road, *c.* 1907. The building from 1888 still looks out over Globe Road but it is now the London Buddhist Centre, the fire-fighters having moved to modern premises close by. The Rising Sun is again seen on the right and there is a glimpse of Bessy Street to the left of the fire station. A pair of postcards by Charles Martin.

Forresters Music Hall, Cambridge (Heath) Road, 1909. Popular entertainment was on offer at this establishment which began life around 1825 as the Artichoke pub before music hall took over in 1889. There were a number of name changes along the way including New Lyric Music Hall and New Lyric Theatre before its conversion in 1912 for cinema performances. The Forresters Super Cinema eventually closed in 1962.

The Northampton Arms, Northampton Street, Cambridge (Heath) Road, c. 1918. Landlord Harry Arundell and his family stand at the doorway of this old corner pub in the small back streets where the Collingwood Estate now stands. Window posters detail the good cheer to be obtained within, including bitter ale at 6d per quart jug and London porter at $3\frac{1}{2}$d – you had to bring your own jug. Meanwhile, a barrel-laden brewer's dray tops up the supply of Truman's Ale.

FROM DARKNESS

TO LIGHT

A postcard produced by the Bethnal Green and East London Housing Association around 1935 to contrast Bethnal Green's housing from the nineteenth and twentieth centuries as flats began to replace many houses in the borough. This process was greatly accelerated with the great municipal rebuilding schemes of the post-war years.

Six

Mile End, Bow and Old Ford

MILE END ROAD.

Mile End Road, c. 1931. The name of the original hamlet of Mile End is derived from its distance, one mile, from Aldgate along the London to Colchester Road. It was an area of open common land where in the Middle Ages Londoners were apt to congregate to enjoy the country air until expanding London absorbed it, but Mile End Road remains spacious and tree-lined. The postcard shows a curiosity, a tiny old shop in the midst of the colonnaded splendour of T. Wickham's drapery store. This was the shop of the watchmaking Spiegelhalter family who began trading in 1828 but refused to sell up when Wickhams wished to build a grand new store – this arrangement has survived the demise of both businesses. To the right is the Empire Cinema whose ancestry is traced back to its days as the Eagle pub and its later development as a music hall called Lusby's and Paragon Music Hall. The postcard reveals that in the 1930s there were still 'West End variety acts three times a day'. The cinema is now called 'Genesis'.

T. Wickham & Sons, draper, nos 69-79 and 85-89 Mile End Road, *c.* 1907. Otto Speigelhalter's clock shop (with the light paint) and ironmonger Edward Hall were already separating the two halves of the Wickham empire but while Mr. Hall sold out to Wickhams for rebuilding, Speigelhalters did not with the results already seen. The Paragon Music Hall, seen before it became the Mile End Empire, lay beyond the shops.

The Vine Tavern, Mile End Road, *c.* 1900. This seventeenth century relic of a once rural Mile End stood on the wide pavement close to Cambridge (Heath) Road until its demolition by Stepney Council in 1903. The busy road traffic upon which the tavern prospered is in evidence on what is a very early example of a photographic postcard. Close by is a bust of Salvation Army founder William Booth marking the beginnings of his mission work on Mile End Waste in 1865.

Mile End Road by Globe Road, *c.* 1906. The Old Globe, a pub which had its origins in the late 1600s still stands on the Globe Road corner but its top floor together with that of neighbouring grocer John Rose & Co. has gone, probably as a result of war damage. Next door, a small weatherboarded property (now rare in the East End) housed William Whitehead, hosier.

Mile End Road by Grafton Street (renamed Grantley Street), *c.* 1906. Ye Old King Harry was another of Mile End Road's hostelries, the monarch here being Henry VIII whose bust surveys the passing scene from a niche on the pub's second floor. Further along, a horse tram is passing the fire station and the Spanish & Portuguese Jew's Hospital whose premises would be rebuilt in 1913. The corner with Grantley Street no longer exists, having been built over by London University's Queen Mary College.

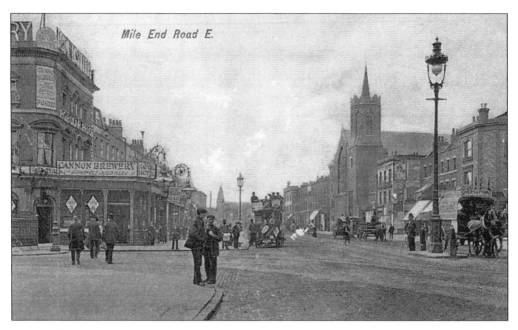

Mile End Road by Burdett Road, c. 1906. The scene was unremarkable in 1906 with the Royal Hotel on the Burdett Road corner and the handsome red-brick Guardian Angels church (1896) visible on the right. Ninety years on, however, there is one of the most extraordinary spectacles in London here as an inspirational green bridge carries the grassland and tall trees of the newly created Mile End Park high above Mile End Road's ceaseless traffic.

Mile End Road near Mile End station, c. 1906. The picture postcard was at the height of its Edwardian popularity when this Charles Martin card was published with its image of E. Bell's shop right, where a placard proclaims the opening of a 'picture postcard showroom' to complement the stock of 'firescreens, art pots, flowers and grasses', The view looks eastward and shows the road surfacing of granite setts which would have given anything other than a tram a rough and noisy ride.

Burdett Road by Baggally Street, 1906. Burdett Road was a product of the 1860s, its construction providing a route between Mile End and the docks and link the east/west highways through the East End. The new street was initially named after the monarch, Victoria, but it was changed to Burdett Road in honour of Baroness Angela Burdett-Coutts the wealthy philanthropist who worked to improve housing conditions in the East End. The character of the road has changed in post-war years with the houses and fire station, left, giving way to the residential Bede Estate while Mile End Park has replaced everything on the right including St Luke's church.

Burdett Road by Bloomfield Road, c. 1909. Bloomfield Road became Bede Road, giving its name in turn to the post-war Bede Estate.

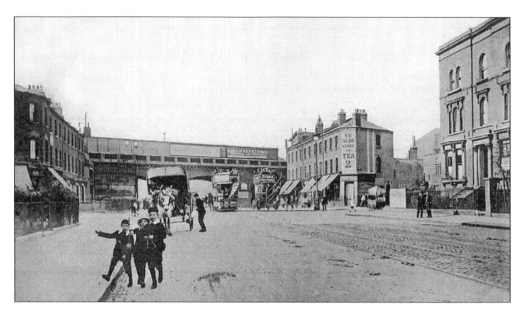

Burdett Road looking towards Mile End, *c.* 1906. The Great Eastern Railway's bridge is still a feature of Burdett Road, but Burdett Road station which adjoined it closed in 1941 following war damage. Here the old shops and houses have given way to modern housing with the towering Elmslie Point, part of the Leopold Estate replacing the shops on the right. On the Turner's Road corner, Charles Heasman's grocery store advertised 'Ye Olde Kynde of Tea', whatever that was!

Grove Road from Mile End Road, *c.* 1906. Grove Road takes Burdett Road's northbound traffic toward Victoria Park and Hackney and there was once a frequent service of horse trams. Today, there is a bus station and an extension to Mile End Park in place of the terraces on the left, but to the right there have been few changes although the Prince of Prussia pub was renamed Prince of Wales, probably due to wartime anti-German sentiment.

Grove Road by Arbery Road, c. 1907. Grove Road has been much altered with post-war housing and extensions to Mile End Park replacing streets of old houses. The Victoria Tavern on the Arbery Road corner displays the typical opulence of the Victorian pub with marbled stonework and flamboyant lanterns but it has been rebuilt in a plainer style.

Grove Road by Arbery Road, c. 1905. One of the Victoria Tavern's lanterns appears on the left with houses beyond which have been replaced by the Newport Estate. Lettering on the distant railway bridge points the way to Coborn Road station which closed in 1946. On 13 June 1944, the bridge was hit by the first flying bomb (Doodle-bug) to land on London, but the bridge was repaired and operational in thirty-six hours.

Bow Road by Addington Road, c. 1910. Mile End Road becomes Bow Road in its eastward progression, the width of the road reflecting its importance as one of London's great highways. The late-Edwardian postcard shows the then new electric tramway which linked Aldgate with Stratford, and Bow Road station, an 1892 resiting of an earlier station. The handsome police station (1903) still stands on the Addington Road corner, left.

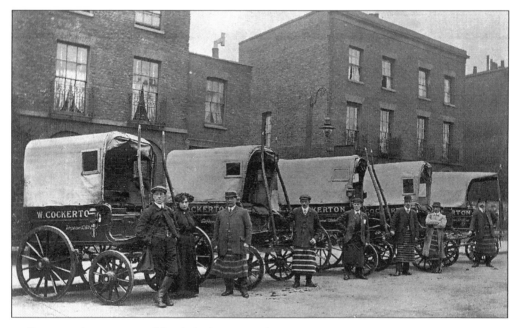

William Cockerton, spiced-beef dealer, 36 Coborn Street, Bow, c. 1910 A postcard of a prospering business in Edwardian Bow with the proprietor, staff and delivery wagons outside their Coborn Street premises. These fine houses built in the 1820s still stand; one of them, no. 30, was the first London address of the young Thomas (Dr.) Barnardo while a student at the London Hospital in 1866.

Bow Church, *c.* 1906. An early motor bus attracts some attention as it passes St Mary's church, the last surviving remnant of medieval Bow, the final village in Middlesex before the highway to Colchester crossed the Lea into Essex. The statue of Victorian Prime Minister Gladstone surveys the scene, but a lost landmark is the Palace Theatre, right, formerly the Three Cups Public House and Music Hall, Marlow's Music Hall, the Eastern Empire and Tivoli Theatre - it ended its days as a cinema. The flats of Bow Bridge Estate are here now.

High Street, Bromley-by-Bow, *c.* 1908. Something of the atmosphere of the village it once was pervaded Edwardian Bromley but nothing here other than the Rose & Crown pub, left, has survived. Bromley-by-Bow was named due to the proximity of the two villages - the High Street now separates the two halves of the Bow Bridge Estate.

Devons Road by Bruce Road, Bromley-by-Bow, *c.* 1908. Devons Road takes a lengthy winding course through Bromley towards Bow Common and featured a typical East End shopping centre and market at the High Street end. The old street patterns vanished with the arrival of the Bow Bridge Estate and Stroudley Walk, an attractively designed shopping and market area.

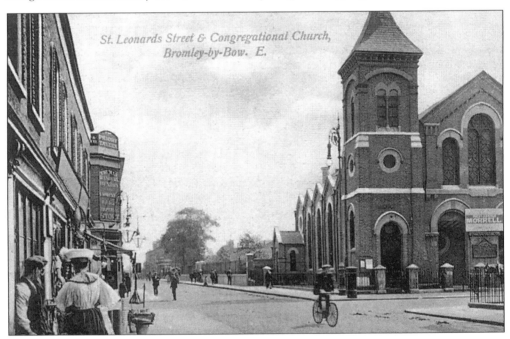

St Leonard's Street, Bromley-by-Bow, *c.* 1908. To the left is the Priory Tavern whose name recalls a long-lost Benedictine Priory dedicated to St Leonard which was founded around AD 1100. The pub was rebuilt before its subsequent closure. Prominently shown is the Bruce Road Congregational church which dated from the 1860s with demolition in 1949 following war damage. A new church was built in 1958 and is now part of a lively community and arts and craft centre.

Potato queue, Devons Road, Bromley-by-Bow, 1917. This amateur photographer's postcard is blurred and grained with the dirt of three-quarters of a century, yet its historic interest earns its place here. It is 1917, and in the grim days of the First World War an acute shortage of potatoes led to ugly scenes at the premises of those grocers fortunate enough to obtain a supply, resulting in a police presence. Here, the queue to Thomas Thackeray's shop stretched past Grace Street and the Duke of Cambridge pub towards Bruce Road. These shops are now a distant memory – the flats of Devons Estate are here now.

A soldier's memorial, Blackthorn Street, 1919. A street memorial to a tragic hero of the First World War, a soldier who did not return to his Blackthorn Street home. Blackthorn Street is now part of the Lincoln (South) Estate.

War damage, Bromley-by-Bow, 1916. The vast aerial bombardment of the Blitz during the Second World War changed the face of the East End for ever, but the Zeppelin and fixed-wing aircraft raids of the First World War also inflicted grievous damage and loss of life. The postcard shows the effect of a high-explosive bomb on local brick and timber housing.

War damage, Bromley-by-Bow, 1916. Shattered rooms and ruined furniture for a family bombed out of a Bromley house during the Zeppelin raids of 1916. These two views are from a long series of wartime postcards featuring the work of prolific East End photographer William Whiffen of East India Dock Road. Others in the set highlight one of the most tragic events of the war, when eighteen children died in a bomb blast at Upper North Street School, Poplar.

Old Ford Road from the 'Skew Bridge', c. 1907. The bridge crosses the Hertford Union Canal (George Duckett's Canal) which was created to link Regent's Canal with the river Lea. The properties on the right have given way to high-rise Ingram House, but the Lord Morpeth pub survives beside it together with a wall plaque which marks the home of two luminaries of the Suffragette movement, Sylvia Pankhurst and Norah Smyth. There was also a 'Women's Hall and Cost Price Restaurant' here from 1914.

Old Ford Road near Old Ford station, c. 1907. The name Old Ford is derived from an early crossing of the river Lea before a more favoured crossing place came into use at Bow Bridge. An animated Charles Martin postcard picturing a section of Old Ford Road later sacrificed for the East Cross Route.

Silver Jubilee street party, Lacy Street off Tredegar Road, 1935. King George V and Queen Mary celebrated the Silver Jubilee of their reign in 1935, and as ever on such occasions there was an outbreak of patriotic fervour and a jolly good East End street party. The sun shone brightly on this gathering of locals and there was musical accompaniment for the inevitable sing-song. Morvill Street runs across the background with the premises of Chandler's Dairy Farm, one of a then dwindling band of urban cow-keepers.

A postcard portrait, c. 1930. Anyone could appear on a postcard, the results of a visit to the photographer's studio being printed in this form for convenient distribution among the subject's family. This study of an unknown East Ender in her bridal finery was an example of the work of Griffiths & Son of Armagh Road, Old Ford.

Mostyn Street (Mostyn Grove since 1939), Tredegar Road, Bow, c. 1907. The street still stands but there is no trace of its old neighbourhood of small houses, local shops and the post office on the Lacy Street corner. The medium-rise flats of the Tredegar Estate are here now.

Charles Lampard's Refreshment Rooms, Roman Road, c. 1905. There was traditional East End fare on offer here with 'Sweeny's noted stewed eels' from one penny a plate, 'superior pea soup' at one penny a bowl and 'hot fried fish' anticipating the ever popular fish and chips. The postcard was sent to Ohio by 'Flo', a member of the Lampard family, 'This is our house and shop'.

Roman Road, *c.* 1912. With its rows of small shops and busy street market, Roman Road remains a vibrant slice of the old East End. The stretch by Ford Road, right, appears little changed but shop fronts have been fitted to the remaining old houses where trading previously took place in the front room. The postcard was written by 'Blanche' from 226 Roman Road, 'do you remember this old spot?'

Roman Road from Parnell Road, *c.* 1906. Shops, market stalls and coster's barrows lined this populous road where according to a contemporary postcard message 'this is where we generally parade night-time. You want to see this road Friday and Saturday nights, market nights, you can't move for people'. The lamp adorning the Hand & Flower pub was a particularly opulent confection.

Seven

East Enders' Transport

The postcard did not arrive in time to record the earliest landmarks in the history of London's transport: the first passenger railway (South London & Greenwich Railway, 1836); the first Underground line (Metropolitan Railway,1863); the first trams (Bayswater Road, 1861) and the first bus route (Marylebone to Bank, 1829). With the nucleus of London's transport system already in place the postcard nevertheless went on to picture the last days of Underground steam traction, the electrification of the trams and the motorization of the buses. In Edwardian times the largest bus fleet was owned by the London General Omnibus Company whose horse drawn and motor-powered vehicles worked alongside those of a variety of other concerns, one of which was the Great Eastern London Motor Omnibus Company. Their service from Upton Park to Oxford Circus usefully linked London's East and West Ends – one of their Straker Squire motors is seen here in Barking Road around 1907.

Horse bus in Roman Road, Old Ford, *c.* 1906. From the time in 1829 that carriage-builder George Shillibeer began London's first bus service, the capital rapidly became connected by an increasing number of routes, horse-drawn buses at first with motors arriving from the early 1900s. The Charles Martin postcard pictures the last decade of the horse bus with an eastward-looking view along Roman Road by Ford Road and a horse drawn forerunner of today's route no. 8.

The Island Omnibus, Glengall Road, *c.* 1906. George Middleditch of West Ferry Road, Isle of Dogs, ran a local service of ten-seater horse buses connecting West India Dock station with West Ferry Road and Millwall Dock Tavern. A further four passengers were accommodated on the roof – they had to hand the driver their fares via a trapdoor in the floor. The home-made postcard pictures an Island bus together with a horse-brake loaded with children as they set off on an outing. Glengall Ironworks looms in the background.

Clarkson steam bus, Poplar, 1908. These buses, which were steam driven and fuelled by paraffin, enjoyed some popularity for the quiet running and useful turn of speed which sometimes tempted their drivers into breaking the 12mph speed limit. This one was photographed with its crew close to its depot at Leven Road, Poplar, from where it served the East End from Canning Town to Aldgate and onward to Hammersmith. (David Brewster collection).

The bus terminus, Stebondale Street by Manchester Road, Cubitt Town, Isle of Dogs, 1925. Here is an example of London's first mass-produced motor bus, the 'B' type, as introduced by the London General Omnibus Company in 1910. The driver attends to his radiator before setting off for distant Mile End on a wet and dreary day which saw all his passengers forsaking the rain-lashed top deck for the seats inside.

An East End bus, c. 1926. A bus crew together with their inspector pose with a red 'General' K type bus which was working route 42 – this took in Tower Bridge, Mile End Gate and Cambridge (Heath) Road. Postcards like these were never sold to the public – they were for the private use of the bus crews who treated them as family photographs.

A 'pirate' bus to Cubitt Town, c. 1929. This smart vehicle served Burdett Road and the Isle of Dogs, the advances of twenty years from the days of the Island horse bus (page 114) being obvious. The 1920s were a colourful decade in the history of London's buses when the red General buses were joined in fierce competition with a new breed of independent or 'pirate' operator vying for the lucrative bus trade. This one was owned by the Peraeque Transport Co. of South London. The 'pirates' disappeared with the creation of London Transport in 1933.

Blackwall Tunnel Approach, Poplar, c. 1913. Another crew and their bus beneath the impressive northern Tunnel House of Blackwall Tunnel. Blackwall was the first road tunnel beneath the Thames, opening in 1897 to ease the cross-Thames traffic which previously had to use London or Tower Bridges. The tunnel was duplicated in 1967 necessitating the removal of the Northern Tunnel House.

Thames passenger boat, c. 1905. On board the *Francis Drake*, one of the LCC's penny steamers which provided a passenger service along the Thames, calling at Wapping, Limehouse and other river piers. The boats offered an enjoyable transport experience but they were not well supported (a problem which has afflicted other river bus services) and it all ended in 1907.

East India Road, (Tram Terminus).

Tram terminus, East India Dock Road by Blackwall Tunnel Approach, *c.* 1905. Horse trams prospered through their ability to carry a greater load of passengers and give them a smoother ride than horse buses could on the cobble-stoned and rolled dirt roads of pre-tarmacadamed London. The first route in the East End, Whitechapel to Bow Bridge, began on 9 May 1870 – others soon followed. This postcard gives a hint of the frequency of the service in 1905 with three cars lined up for the journey to Aldgate or Bloomsbury.

Trams at the Eastern Hotel, East and West India Dock Roads, *c.* 1913. An amateur photographer's postcard captures the last of the East End's horse tram routes, West India Dock to South Hackney, which ceased in 1914 when the horses were requisitioned for army service at the beginning of the First World War. Electric trams running towards the Essex suburbs are seen on the left.

Experimental electric tram, Mile End Road by Grove Buildings, 1908. London's first electric trams made their appearance in 1901 and soon began to replace their horse drawn predecessors, the electricity which powered them being gathered either via a trolley pole and overhead wire or a channel (conduit) set between the running rails. A third, experimental, method, the GB Surface Contact System, was tried briefly in Whitechapel and Mile End Roads – this consisted of electrically charged 'studs' on the road surface, the current being picked up by the tram as it passed over them. The first fare-paying passengers made their journeys on 25 June 1908 and were duly impressed by the smooth running and rapid acceleration of the tramcars, but problems arose when they caught up with the horse trams which continued to share the rails. Fears were also voiced over the proximity of 'live studs' to other road users, misgivings which were soon realised when a horse pulling a cart belonging to Messrs. J.J. Prior & Co., contractors to Stepney Borough Council, slipped and fell onto a live stud and was rendered unfit for further work. Another car gave its passengers a fright when it caught fire, while others sometimes became stranded between studs and had to be pushed to the next one. The whole experiment degenerated into a fiasco and after around six months the East End breathed a sigh of relief as the scheme was abandoned due to its 'inability to withstand heavy traffic and London mud'. The lines returned to horse traction before being electrified by more conventional means. The postcard by an unknown photographer catches an Aldgate-bound 'stud-tram' close to the Plough pub while a knife-grinder, a relic of an earlier age, plies his trade on the pavement, right.

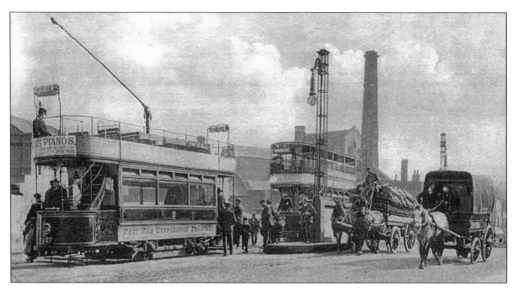

Electric trams at Bow Bridge, c. 1908. Bow Bridge crossed the river Lea at the historic boundaries of the counties of Middlesex and Essex, the Metropolitan Boroughs of Poplar and West Ham and latterly, the London Boroughs of Tower Hamlets and Newham. Bow was an important transport interchange with its wealth of railway stations, tram lines and bus routes, and busy scenes like this were commonplace. The second tram is sporting a covered top deck, an improvement which would take motor buses another twenty years to adopt in any quantity.

An East End trolley bus, Smithfield. Trams began to be replaced by trolleybuses from the 1930s and were highly popular due to their smooth silent running when compared with the ground-shaking vibrations of the trams. They nevertheless had a short life, finally disappearing from the London scene in May 1962 leaving motor buses to rule the roads. This trolley's route took it to Aldgate, Commercial Road, Limehouse and onward to Barking.

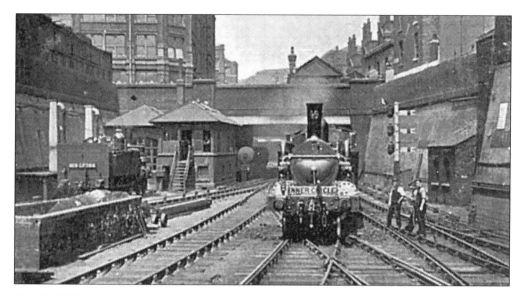

Outside Aldgate station, *c.* 1903. An extension of the world's first underground passenger railway, the Metropolitan which began running in 1863, reached Aldgate in 1876. There were still steam-hauled trains working the lines in the early 1900s despite problems caused by the locomotive's emissions in the tunnels. The postcard by the Locomotive Publishing Co (which specialised in railway themes) shows a steam train on the Inner Circle line with Gravel Lane in the background.

Aldgate East station, Whitechapel High Street by Goulston Street, *c.* 1915. The station opened for business on 6 October 1884 serving the District and Metropolitan lines - one of the station entrances was resited to its present position by Commercial Street in 1938. The postcard by S. Eisner & Son of Whitechapel High Street looks westwards along Aldgate High Street and shows the tower of St Botolph's church, and on the Middlesex Street corner, the Essex pub with its clock.

East London Railway staff at Wapping station, 1910. The East London Railway Company opened its station at Wapping on 7 December 1869, the line running southwards from here to New Cross via Brunel's pioneering Thames Tunnel which opened in 1843. The railway was electrified in 1913 for the Metropolitan line and the wooden station building was rebuilt (also in wood) in 1915. A new station opened in 1960 replacing a temporary structure used since wartime. (Keith Nickol Collection).

Shadwell & St George-in-the-East station, Watney Street, c. 1910. This East London Railway station gained its lengthy name in 1900 but in 1918 it reverted to 'Shadwell', the name it was given when it opened in 1876. The simple brick-built station can still be seen but with a new entrance in Cable Street and an interchange with the Docklands Light Railway. A Great Eastern Railway poster on the wall was partly written in Yiddish for the local Jewish population. (Paul Laming Collection).

Opposite: Postcards issued by railway companies to publicise places of interest close to their stations are known as Railway Officials. This one is part of a series called London Nooks and Corners and features picturesque scenes close to the East London Railway. The richly hued watercolours picture Wapping parish church; Wapping Old Stairs; old buildings in Aldgate High Street with the Prospect of Whitby and the Dockmaster's House, both at Shadwell. The portrait is of Admiral Sir John Leeke who is buried at Rotherhithe.

UNDERGROUND

EAST LON-DON.

Sir John Leeke

WAPPING OLD STAIRS

WAPPING CHURCH

BUTCHERS SHOPS AT ALDGATE

DOCKMASTER'S HOUSE. SHADWELL

PROSPECT OF WHITBY. SHADWELL

S.T.C.WEEKS

Fenchurch Street station, *c.* 1906. The London & Blackwall Railway built an impressive viaduct high above the streets of Limehouse and Shadwell to terminate initially at Minories on the City boundary, and then into the City itself at Fenchurch Street in 1841. The future site of the Docklands Light Railway's Tower Gateway station lays in the centre distance of this Locomotive Publishing Company view.

The Great Eastern Railway Company's vast complex of lines on their viaduct at the point where it crosses Vallance Road, Bethnal Green. Passenger services used the lines on the right and are seen as they begin the gentle descent to the Liverpool Street terminus. Freight services were to the left, the tracks leading into Bishopsgate Goods station. A postcard from around 1906 by the Locomotive Publishing Company.

Bishopsgate Goods station, Shoreditch High Street, *c.* 1905. The Great Eastern Railway's goods station was built in 1881 on the site of one of the capital's earliest termini, the Eastern Counties Railway's 'London' station of 1840, which was used for passenger traffic until Liverpool Street station opened in 1874. This Shadow Catchers postcard shows a small part of the vast complex which closed following a fire in 1964 but still contains brick arches from around 1839, some of the world's oldest surviving railway constructions.

Shoredith station, Kingsland Road by Old Street, *c.* 1905. A fine image by the City Studios of a station which was opened by the North London Railway in 1865 and closed in 1940. The neighbouring Spread Eagle pub held a music hall license in Victorian times while next door, William Stevens, whip maker, offered a useful service in horse-drawn London.

South Dock station, Isle of Dogs, *c.* 1906. The London, Blackwall & Millwall Extension Railway opened in December 1871 to serve the new Millwall Docks and to link Fenchurch Street with the Thames ferries at the tip of the Isle of Dogs. Some of the bridges along the new line were of such flimsy construction that steam locomotives were considered too dangerous and horses hauled the trains at first. This wooden station was surrounded by the waters of the docks.

North Greenwich & Cubitt Town station, *c.* 1905. The railway was extended from Millwall Docks to this riverside terminus in July 1872 by means of an impressive brick viaduct. The railway closed in 1926 but the arches of the viaduct proved useful as air raid shelters during the Second World War and the viaduct was revived with the opening of the Docklands Light Railway in 1987. Island Gardens are here now.

Bow station, c. 1907. The North London Railway's station at Bow opened in 1850 and closed in 1944, the trains from here linking such diverse areas of London as Hampstead and Kew – there was a City terminus at Broad Street. The station presented a grand frontage to Bow Road and there was a meeting hall, the Bow and Bromley Institute, on the top floor. The building ended its days as Bow Palais de Danse until fire destroyed it around 1957.

Bow Road station, c. 1906. The first of the Great Eastern Railway's stations at Bow Road opened in 1876 and closed in 1892 when its successor, seen here, opened. This lasted until 1949 but the building lives on as a betting shop. The prominent route details displayed on the bridge were typical of Victorian and Edwardian days. A pair of postcards by Charles Martin.

Victoria Park, c. 1906. The East End was not all bricks and industry, the sometimes seemingly endless streets being relieved by this, one of London's finest municipal parks. Victoria Park was opened in 1845, its area including the site of the ancient Manor House of Stepney which was demolished in 1800. The bathing lake was a popular attraction for young East Enders as may be seen on this postcard, part of a local set produced by A. Day's photographic studio, Hackney.

Acknowledgements

For their kindness in allowing me to include postcards from their personal collections, special thanks are due to: Ann Harris, Maurice Friedman, David Brewster, Paul Laming and Keith Nickol and to Judges Postcards, Hastings, for the use of images which are their copyright. A very big 'thank you' as well to R.W. Kidner, Ray Newton and Steve Kentfield for their specialised knowledge and to Tower Hamlets Local History and Archives, (Bancroft Road Library) and Guildhall Library, City of London for the use of their facilities.

Books consulted include:
London Docklands, Elizabeth Williamson and Nikolaus Pevsner; *Exploring the East End*, Rosemary Taylor; *The East End Then and Now*, Winston G. Ramsey; *London Theatres and Music Halls*, Diana Howard; *The Hamlets and the Tower*, David Rich; *A Riverside Journey*, Steve Kentfield and Ray Newton; *Aldgate and Stepney Tramways*, Robert J. Hurley and *The Isle of Dogs 1066–1918*, Eve Hostettler.

Printed in Germany
by Amazon Distribution
GmbH, Leipzig

19484956R00075